MW00512268

The
Unveiling
Of The Trinity

A Biblical Account of the Mystery Revealed

Tom Bosse

Tuvott Publishing

The Unveiling of the Trinity
All Scripture quotations are taken from the King James Version of the Bible.
Note: Tuvott Publishing's style of capitalizing certain Scripture pronouns that refer
to the Father, Son and Holy Ghost and may differ from other Bible publishing styles.

Library of Congress Control Number: 2002094445
ISBN 0-9723974-0-X

© Cover Design by: mooregraphix@fuse.net

Published by
Tuvott Publishing
PO Box 18276
Erlanger, KY 41018-0276
www.tuvott.com

PRINTED IN THE UNITED STATES OF AMERICA

Acknowledgements

A particular thanks to three special ladies who took time to help with the fine points of this book.

Marion Duebel - thanks for your patience and persistance and keen perception to detail.
Valerie Snebold - thanks for being there with your credentials of wisdom and knowledge.
Kimberly Sinning - thanks for your involvement which was invaluable with the finishing touches.

Also a specific word of thanks to Professor Larry Duebel for his dedication and sound advice.

To my wife and children for patients and understanding during the production of this book.

Come ye near unto Me, hear ye this: I have not spoken in secret from the beginning; from the time that it was, there *am* I: and now the Lord God, and His Spirit, hath sent Me. - (Isaiah 48:16)

Contents

Introduction

What is the Trinity? For many, it's simply a mystery that no one can explain. Untold pages have been written attempting to shed some light on its meaning, without much success. History has recorded its perplexities, councils were set up to justify its validity, and time has delivered more questions than answers. How is it possible for God the Father to be in heaven, while God the Son was walking on the earth? How could God the Father and God the Son be in heaven, while God the Holy Ghost is dwelling in the hearts of men down on the earth? Is it possible for a man named Jesus to also be God? These are some of the questions that have remained undefined. Even in this super information age, there continues to be no clear identifiable understanding of this vital Church doctrine.

The purpose of this book is to establish a foundation to launch the unveiling of the Trinity. In the religious communities, both Christian and non-Christian, there seems to be a great deal of misunderstanding when it comes to the Trinity. For example, the religion of Judaism has a concern with the three persons in one God because it seems to disagree with Deuteronomy 6:4, which says, "Hear O Israel: The Lord our God is one Lord." Some religious groups believe Jesus was a prophet, a good teacher, or simply a good man but certainly not God in the flesh. Nevertheless, there are even some religions, which label themselves Christian, but claim that Jesus was an angel or a god. What truly seems to trigger this misunderstanding of the Trinity are a couple of questions previously mentioned. First: How can God be manifested in three persons if He is one God? Second: How can Jesus be fully God and fully man?

Why has the Trinity been one of the most difficult doctrines of the Church to understand? Even theologians are seemingly at a loss trying to comprehend the elementary concept that defines the Trinity? They know what the Trinity is, but are unable to explain it in a practical way, leaving many confused.

The contents of this book are structured in such a way to take you on a step by step adventure into the vast empire of who God is with respect to His complete Godhead. God did not intend for His attributes to be hidden from us. The Bible is full of God's personality and character, and they are open and visible to us when we seek them. Needless to say, the answers were there all the time. We simply overlooked them without giving closer analysis of the many Scripture verses concerning this subject matter.

Are you are among those confused about the Trinity? As you read this book, it will open a door of new encounters in your study of the Bible. As we approach the end of this age, God is revealing many things to man concerning His Word. If we are to keep abreast of His revelation for our lives, we must make His Word our first interest in this fast paced world.

Understanding the Trinity, and understanding who Christ is, will unlock greater insights into all Scriptures, not only in the New Testament, but the Old Testament as well. Because the Trinity is related to many other questionable concerns, those issues will also become apparent. You shall see how the relationship of the Father, the Son, and the Holy Ghost is truly One. You will understand Colossians 2:9, which says, "For in Him dwells all the fullness of the Godhead bodily."

The Author

"What Jesus Means to Me"

He's my Hotline to the Father,
He's my Comforter when I feel depressed,
He's my Lawyer when I'm in trouble,
He's my Peace when I need some rest,

He's my Joy when I feel like dancing,
He's my Physician when I don't feel well,
He's my Friend when I need a partner,
And He saved me from the pits of Hell,

He's always there just when I need Him,
He makes me to laugh, He makes me to cry,
And I know He will never leave me,
Even till the day that I die.

Chapter 1

Objective, Design and History

The Journey of Life:
Have you ever considered yourself a traveler in time? In reality, that is what we are. As preceding generations have gone before, it is our turn to take the journey of life on this planet called earth. Every day those who have completed their journey disembark, while new travelers climb aboard for their trip. At this time, several billion people are taking the trip together. As these individuals make their pilgrimage down life's pathway— are they truly mindful of the purpose for their journey? Is it only by chance they are here? Could it be a coincidence they happened to be here at this time in history? The time allotted to fulfill their journey is uncertain. Just when or where the journey will conclude is unknown. All the same, one thing *is* certain, there will be an end to the journey.

Traveling through life takes on many unusual distinctions. For some individuals, life is like being on a treadmill. They walk and walk, but get nowhere. Others turn the speed up so fast that their life is half over before they know where they have been. The pleasures and attractions of life can grab our attention. The troubles and cares of the world often capture our concerns. Life is full of distractions, and for that reason we must get our focus on the important things that matter. In this book, we shall find that there is no better subject than the Trinity to bring into perspective the important things of life.

While the Trinity relates to the doctrine of the Godhead, its main purpose is life. Because of that fact, considering we are all on this expedition called life, no other topic demands the notability for our existence than does the Trinity. Stated another way—when we think of this journey on earth as a testing period, there is only one way to pass the test and that is through the principles contained in the Trinity.

The Concept of the Trinity:

The concept of the Trinity is truly hard for some to understand. The accepted perception is one of confusion and mysticism. Often the Trinity is presented in such a complex way that the end result only brings added confusion. Despite that, the Bible relates that God is not the author of confusion.

Briefly, the requirement for an incarnate God came about as a result of man's disobedience to God's decree. The biblical account of Adam and Eve in the "Garden of Eden" gives details relating to the disobedience. Their disobedience brought about death in man, and death ushered in the need for a Savior. The incarnate God became the Savior, and the Savior became the heart of the Trinity. Since the Savior conquered death, hell, and the grave, God also established a way for man to experience unconditional new life again. However, even though the new life is unconditional—that is, it has no strings attached—it is provisional, meaning it is available only through the Savior.

The Trinity is stated as fact in Scripture. For that reason, it was never presented as a topic. The Bible assumes it; therefore, because it is not stated, many simply regard it as non-existing. On the other hand, another issue emerges to those who accept the Trinity as fact. While much evidence is supplied in Scripture to support its accuracy, many believers fail to see the relationship of the three individual persons of God. This is one place where complexity could play a role.

Reaching Our Destination:

Before we venture too far, a few details about our destination and how we intend to get there will prove beneficial. We have structured this study to provide a full illustration of what the Trinity is. First, though, the pieces of the illustration must be assembled together. Some things we shall find to be familiar and some, unfamiliar. By gathering a background of information, we will be ready to put the final touches on the overall picture. Scripture verses are the staple of our study, and many are represented in the research of our topic.

To begin this chapter of our study, we will take a brief look at the meaning and definition of the Trinity. In like fashion, an investigation of the Trinity's historical background will reveal its origin. These and a few other particulars shall provide us with the vital information to build upon.

You will find throughout this book that many words attributed to the Godhead are capitalized. This is to establish a contrast between the fundamental nature of mortal man and the deified nature ascribed to God.

Seeing the Completed Picture:

Each chapter of this book contains helpful information. It is this information that will assist us in formulating a clear and concise picture of the Trinity. For that reason, a thorough covering of the material is necessary. In Luke's gospel is recorded a prayer of Jesus. This prayer shows us that the only way we can learn the truths of God is when He reveals them to us.

- In that hour Jesus rejoiced in spirit, and said, I thank Thee, O Father, Lord of heaven and earth, that Thou hast hid these things from the wise and prudent, and hast revealed them unto babes: even so, Father; for so it seemed good in Thy sight. - (Luke 10:21)

11

- All things are delivered to Me of My Father: and no man knoweth who the Son is, but the Father; and who the Father is, but the Son, and *he* to whom the Son will reveal *Him*. - (Luke 10:22)

How the Trinity is Defined:
The Trinity is a distinctive doctrine, which declares that one God exists in three Persons. These three manifestations of God are presented in the Bible as the Father, the Son (Jesus Christ) and the Holy Ghost (sometimes referred to as the Holy Spirit). They are not three different people, but they are expressed as three Persons in one God, or one God revealed in three ways.

When the Bible mentions God, it generally refers to God as *the Father*. Nevertheless, references are also found regarding *Jesus* and *the Holy Spirit* as God. The word Trinity is not found in Scripture, and its reference is established in only one particular place in the Bible as follows:

- Go ye therefore, and teach all nations, baptizing them in the name of the Father, and of the Son, and of the Holy Ghost: - (Matthew 28:19)

Within the boundaries of this verse of Scripture, Jesus also bestowed the command of *the Great Commission* upon His disciples. This specific passage provides us with a view of the Godhead, along with the relationship linking one to another.

Additional Trinity Scriptures:
While the Trinity is defined in only one verse, we can find other Scriptures in both the Old and New Testaments that expound on the three manifestations of one God. The Old Testament book of Isaiah contains one such verse. This passage makes it evident that God is talking as the second Person of the Godhead:

- Come ye near unto Me, hear ye this; I have not spoken in secret from the beginning; from the time that it was, there *am* I: and now the Lord God, and His Spirit, hath sent Me. - (Isaiah 48:16)

Here we have God speaking as the second Person (God the Son) saying, "Come ye near Me (God the Son), hear ye this; I have not spoken in secret from the beginning; from the time that it was, there *am* I (God the Son): and now the Lord God (the Father), and His Spirit (God the Holy Spirit), hath sent Me (God the Son)."

In the gospel of Luke we find John the Baptist baptizing Jesus, and we are presented with the following illustration:

- Now when all the people were baptized, it came to pass, that Jesus also being baptized, and praying, the heaven was opened, - (Luke 3:21)
- And the Holy Ghost descended in a bodily shape like a dove upon Him, and a voice came from heaven, which said, Thou art My beloved Son; in Thee I am well pleased. - (Luke 3: 22)

Notice the Trinity in the preceding passage. Jesus is being baptized, the voice of the Father is in heaven, and the Holy Ghost descends upon Jesus like a dove.

Let's look at one more example where the entire Godhead is represented within the same passage. The Last Supper has just ended, and Jesus makes this statement to His disciples:

- But when the Comforter is come, whom I will send unto you from the Father, *even* the Spirit of truth, which proceedeth from the Father, He shall testify of Me: - (John 15:26)

13

In this Scripture, the word Comforter is another name for the Holy Spirit. Here we see Jesus talking about sending the Holy Spirit from the Father. This too reveals the entire Godhead in just one verse. There are several other Scripture passages available illustrating the entire Godhead, but these will be adequate for our purposes.

Explaining the Trinity:
Defining the Trinity seems to be an easier task than explaining it. On the whole, the necessity of explaining it has resulted in a loss of words for many. There have been numerous well-intended definitions and analogies attempted, yet they remain as futile efforts without giving a reasonable explanation. The main view, commonly used for explanation, is the one handed down from the Nicene Council in the fourth century A.D. Still and all, even that view does not render a full disclosure of the composition of the Godhead.

Religions Reject the Trinity:
All world religions, except one, completely reject the concept of the Trinity. The focal point of this rejection centers mainly on the refusal to acknowledge the deity of Jesus Christ. Christianity is the only religion to incorporate the Trinity into its belief system. Christians embrace the Trinity to the extent it is the most important tenet of their Faith. The reasoning maintains that if Jesus were not God, Christianity would be like most other religions, seeking after a man.

Judaism is the only other religion to share the same God as Christianity. While they believe in God the Father, they too reject the deity of Jesus Christ. However, they do accept the Holy Spirit, but not with the same distinction as projected by Christendom. Judaism's conflict with the Trinity stems from the Scripture in Deuteronomy 6:4, which states: "Hear, O Israel: The LORD our God is one LORD."

The Documents Unchanged:
It was during the first centuries that the Church constructed and introduced the contents of the Trinity. Although they have been debated and scrutinized over the years, these documents remain practically the same to this day. A hidden element within the Trinity obscured its full disclosure. Hence, the view of the Church is that the Trinity is beyond man's full comprehension.

The Need for Understanding:
The absence of understanding regarding the topic of the Trinity has definitely kept many away from the Christian religion. The question arises: If confusion exists among the Christian Church leaders pertaining to such a vital doctrine as this, why then would I want to join one of them. Consequently, many who are searching for something to satisfy the spiritual appetite in their lives have looked elsewhere for answers.

Early Church History:
Much of early Church history is associated with the Trinity, yet there was no mention of the word Trinity by the New Testament writers in their transcripts. It was not until the second century that the word Trinity was first introduced. As it happened, disagreements followed its teaching almost immediately. Needless to say, these differences of opinion sparked many arguments regarding its creed.

After finally establishing itself as a major doctrine, another conflict developed in the fourth century. This came about through a teaching by a man named *Arius* (256-336 A.D.), intending to cast doubt upon the divinity of Jesus Christ.

Many embraced *Arius's* teaching, which became known as *Arianism*. His view taught that since Jesus was begotten and created, He could not have been God, for God was neither begotten, nor had a beginning.

To combat this heresy, and to set up doctrinal guidelines to be followed, the Church called for a conclave of bishops. This occurred in 325 A.D. and is known as *the First Council of Nicaea*. This is the council that produced the "Nicene Creed." The council reinforced the Church's stand, proclaiming Jesus as both God and Man.

Even after the *Nicaea Council* asserted its position, acknowledging the full deity of Christ, *Arianism* continued to attract followers for several years, and traces of the teaching remains even to this day.

Other Councils and Committees:
A second council was held in 381 A.D. at Constantinople to help strengthen the position instituted at Nicene. It also established the fullness of the Holy Spirit and His position in the Godhead. Other councils formed later to reinforce the views created at Nicene and Constantinople. Primarily, each council upheld the deity of Jesus and affirmed the divinity of the Holy Spirit to be of the same nature as the Father and the Son.

The documents produced by these council meetings have shaped the beliefs shared by most Christian churches. In general, these beliefs acknowledge that the Father is God Almighty, Creator of heaven and earth. Jesus is His only begotten Son, begotten not made, one with the Father. The Holy Ghost is the Lord and giver of life, who proceeds from the Father and the Son. This teaching is identical to the one in operation by the Church today in describing the Trinity.

Differences of Understanding:
Since the apostolic days of a united Church, divisions have occurred within Christianity. Those divisions generally came about due to disagreements regarding the interpretation of the Scriptures or in disobedience to the governing authorities.

Throughout the years, several denominations have formed as a result of those differences. Still, despite the differences, most of these denominations agree on nearly all areas of doctrine, including the Trinity.

Some Denominations Reject the Trinity:

A few denominations, which look upon themselves as Christian, have denounced the Trinity altogether. Their view on the Trinity generally lines up with many non-Christian religions. Because they have incorporated Jesus into their religious structure, these organizations operate under the umbrella of Christianity. Since their teachings are contrary to what mainline Churches teach about the Trinity, they are viewed as outside the mainstream.

Non-Christian Inquiry:

Some non-Christian religions have attempted to analyze the Trinity to see if it would fit in with any of their beliefs. In particular, because Jesus Christ is God and Man, not one religion could justify His deity. Still, the many religions in the world today have produced a wide assortment of beliefs centered on ideas from man.

The irony of a non-Christian religion professing a belief in Christ is that their identity would cease to be catalogued under a non-Christian name. By professing a belief in Christ, their classification would appear under the heading of Christianity.

A Later Chapter Report on Religions:

In a later chapter, we shall take a look at some of the more popular world religions and what their teachings involve. This information will prove to be valuable in several ways. Not only will it provide a comparison of the different belief systems, but it will also illustrate how each religious system presents the Trinity to its followers.

An Overview of Chapter One:

Now let's take a look at some of the issues covered in this chapter. Everyone must take the journey called life. However, that journey will one day come to an abrupt end for each person. The attractions of this life are not the most important thing, but the caring for our soul. What does life have to do with the Trinity? Contained within the Trinity we find the very essence of life. Scripture does not present the Trinity as a topic, but the evidence contained in Scripture assumes it as fact.

A careful and thorough reading of this study is necessary to realize the entire picture of the Trinity. The only place in the Bible where we exclusively find the Father, Son and Holy Ghost mentioned is in Matthew 28:19. The Trinity is distinctive to the Christian faith. This doctrine is of the utmost importance to the Church. If Jesus were not part of the Godhead, Christianity would be like many other religions.

Controversy has followed the study of the Trinity since early in Church history. A disagreement relating to the divinity of Jesus became a major stumbling block concerning the Trinity. From the onset, man has had a problem understanding the make-up of the Trinity because of its obscure nature. Most mainline Christian denominations generally use the description of the Trinity as put forth by the Nicene Council.

Chapter 2

Purpose and Importance

The Trinity—Beyond Belief?

A question from the casual observer might be: Is the Trinity really that important? The obvious reply from a non-believer's viewpoint would be a definite *no*. Other religions get along fine without it, so what is the big deal? Yes, the concept of a God-Man may be hard for the natural mind to conceive. At the same time, the Holy Spirit, dwelling in the hearts of men, may be looked upon as unthinkable by some.

For those who hold fast to certain values and ideas of their own, a teaching of this nature may truly seem odd. In reality, it is no more unusual than what other religions believe and profess. The difference comes into focus when the Spirit of God takes up residence within a person's life, because then the evidence becomes real. This fact expresses one reason why the Trinity is so essential. As we progress further in our readings we shall address this detail in greater depth, but for now, let's look at the significance of the Trinity from a different viewpoint.

No Other Like Him in History:

So then, is the Trinity really that important? In simple terms, consider this: When we say that the Trinity is of no value it means we are still dead in our sins. The Trinity is not only the essence of God, but it is also the root of our eternal salvation.

The second Person of the Trinity (Jesus Christ) made some very forthright proclamations about Himself and about salvation. Jesus reported in John 10:30, "I and *My* Father are One." No other person in the history of humanity ever made such bold statements and authenticated those statements with healings and miracles as did this Man.

He restored the eyes of the blind, the ears of the deaf, and the tongue of the dumb. He healed the sick, cleansed the leper and raised the dead. He willingly gave His life to redeem humanity back to God. Many recorded His deeds, and many chose martyrdom over denying Him. He plainly laid everything out before us, not hiding anything.

A Decision Must be Made:

How do the statements made by Jesus affect us as individuals? What if we choose not to believe what He said? How about our education or riches? Well, for one thing, a decision will be performed regardless of whether we believe or not. Moreover, our background or status in life renders little substance at this point. We can ignore Him and everything He said, or we can accept Him and receive what He said as truth. We can question: Is He really who He says He is, or is He an impostor? Despite that, no matter how we believe, a decision has already been made in our heart.

Clearly, if Jesus said He was only a man, instead of making Himself equal with God, things would be different. The choice would have been much easier to resolve. By making the statement that He is equal with the Father, also gives new meaning to our decision. Needless to say, every person who passes through this earthly journey shall come face to face with this vital issue. What it comes down to is this: If what Jesus said is true and we reject the Trinity, we are also rejecting Jesus; in turn, if we reject Jesus, we also reject the Father.

After careful study, and in light of our eternal destiny, the impact of making the right choice becomes evident. We control our fate by our own free will. Considering how important this decision really is, it should be made only after a thorough and exhaustive examination. Besides, we must take into account that finding realistic answers is vital in making this choice.

Finding Realistic Answers:

Imagine a ball team playing a game without any knowledge of the rules, or a regiment of soldiers fighting in a war without any basic training. Of course it would be disastrous in both cases. In the same way, if God permitted man to go about life on earth without any directives, it would also be chaotic. However, that was not the case. God provided certain standards for us to live by so we might enjoy a full and fruitful existence. By obeying these principles we can avoid the pitfalls of life.

Obviously, only by *obeying* the rules can we overcome the problems and challenges that we face daily. Yet, if we begin searching for answers to these problems and challenges in the wrong places, we should expect to meet with difficulties. The Bible says, "...let God be true, but every man a liar..." Romans 3:4. We must be realistic about what constitutes answers and where those answers are found.

Answers to Questions:

We find that certain questions can be answered because they are unchanging in nature. An example is the problem 2+2=4. We know it never changes; it will always be the same answer. There are also questions that may have several answers, any one of which could be correct. The following is an example of this type of question: "How do I get to a certain city from a particular starting point?" In this example, you may be able to reach the destination by taking several different roads. Thus, several answers could be right for the same question.

We find that many answers to questions come specifically from man's perspective. For example, encyclopedias or textbooks are places to find answers relating to typical technical, historical, geographical or genealogical questions. Many times only one person will supply those answers, rendering only one viewpoint. Because people sometimes perceive things differently, it is improbable that two people would write about the same topic in exactly the same way. Thus, when a topic is developed from the viewpoint of only one person, that one person's opinion is all we have to go by.

Shall We Trust Our Judgment:

Another example to consider, in this day of limitless communications, is journalism. What we see or hear from the news media today is perhaps what a certain journalist might observe regarding a particular situation. What he passes on to us is how we perceive the matter to be. The main concern here relates to what the journalist is conveying to us. His perception of an incident might not be what is really happening.

Two men appear to be fighting, but when the journalist turns his back and leaves the area, the two men show that they were just playing and laughingly hug each other. The journalist was honestly reporting what he saw and was relaying his version of it to us. However, if he had stayed on the scene one more minute, the story would have been entirely different. As was true for the journalist, anything we see or hear might not really be what we think it is. Men make mistakes.

Where to Find Realistic Answers:

A person's ability to tell a lie presents another concern. The Scripture we read earlier "...let God be true but every man a liar..." recorded in Roman's 3:4 specifies that concern. Finding one man who has never told a lie would be quite an effort.

For some individuals, lies are useful to promote a cause or to deceive someone into giving or joining a certain organization. Lies become contagious. One lie may be covering up another wrong, therefore caution is always necessary whenever we are called upon to accept what we read or hear. That is, unless the answer is of a static nature (like 2+2=4).

The possibility for error exists even with the best of intentions. Accordingly, we should consider questions and answers relating to God and our eternal destiny with careful thought as to their content and source.

The Word of God is the one place to find realistic answers; in addition, we have the assurance that its content is of a static nature. His Word never changes; it always remains the same. Jesus said, "Heaven and earth shall pass away, but my Words shall not pass away," Matthew 24:35.

Biblical Truths:

The Bible represents the primary source for information contained in this book. Written within the pages of the Bible are the mysteries of life, along with the purposes and goals appointed to mankind. Moreover, the Bible discloses man's earthly existence, from his beginnings in Genesis, to his end in Revelation. It announces the full allotted time of man as well as his relationship with God. Death, hell and the grave are its judgments. Heaven, grace and eternal life are its rewards.

The Old Testament segment of the Bible includes the same Holy Scriptures as used by the religion of Judaism. The New Testament, like the Trinity, is unique to the Christian religion. These two Testaments, appropriately called the "Word of God," are considered by many to be the only absolutes in the world today. The Bible has withstood both time and testing. This becomes obvious when we consider the following:

1. It would take only one lie in the whole Word of God to discount every other word between its covers.
2. If there is one untruth, or one contradiction, within its pages, then you should discard the whole Book. Who knows, if there is one untruth, there could very well be another, and if another, which one is it?

Hence, you can readily see the ever-increasing implications with this type of reasoning. On that basis, we believe the Bible to be all Truth and the source of all Truth.

The Problem of Understanding Scripture:

Since the Bible is a spiritual book, its contents can be hard to understand when encountered by the secular mind. The earthly mind is not in tune with spiritual expressions, particularly those concerning doctrinal truths. Misunderstanding can cause confusion, and confusion sometimes leads to disbelief. Because the Bible is a spiritual book and written for the spiritually minded, it is only through the Spirit of God that one can realize the Word of God. For a better understanding of this reality, consider the following Scripture:

- But the natural man receiveth not the things of the Spirit of God: for they are foolishness unto him: neither can he know *them*, because they are spiritually discerned - (1 Cor. 1:14)

The Trinity underscores how man receives the Spirit of God, and by receiving the Spirit of God, we are capable of understanding the Word of God.

The Heart of the Trinity is the Love of God:

Here is one more important reason for the Trinity. Many times we envision God as someone standing in heaven just waiting for us to do something wrong so He can punish us. While it may be true that God is a just God, the Bible also reveals God as tolerant and long-suffering. He knows we are but flesh and offers us many chances in life. The Bible calls Him a loving God, and that love is contained in the very heart of the Trinity.

Looking Ahead:
In these first two chapters, we touched on the purpose, history and importance of the Trinity. In our next few lessons, we will take a closer look at man, what he worships, his make-up, as well as his relationship with God. We shall find that the Trinity pertains not only to God, but its significance applies also to man. The very essence of the Trinity presents man as its chief concern. Why? One reason could be that man is the only creature made in the image and likeness of God.

The Egg and the Water:
The following are a couple of examples intended to teach us how to understand the makeup of the Trinity. These examples were a major factor that stimulated the writing of this book. In our first example, the preacher's message arrived at a point where he needed to explain the Trinity. His explanation went like this: "The Trinity can be compared to an egg, whereas the shell represents God the Father, the yolk represents God the Son, and the white represents God the Holy Ghost."

Some time later another preacher donated this description. He was using a different version of analogy by comparing the Trinity to the three stages of water. In this illustration, the liquid represented God the Father, the ice represented God the Son, and the steam represented God the Holy Spirit.

Perhaps you have heard these comparisons yourself at some point. They represent only two of the many examples in existence today attempting to explain the Trinity. Where did these ideas come from? Could analogies be the only way to explain the Trinity? These ideas seem incredibly reasonable, especially to those resigned to the fact that the Trinity shall always remain a mystery.

In Summary of Chapter Two:

The idea of the Trinity may seem ridiculous to some who profess another belief system. In actuality, when the Spirit of God comes to live in a person's life, the evidence becomes real. The Trinity is the very essence of the Godhead and the basis of deliverance. No other person in history has ever made such bold statements as Jesus did about His position in the Godhead and backed up His remarks with miracles and healings of every kind. Therefore, every individual must make a choice.

We can ignore Him, reject Him or accept Him. Man has a free will; hence, whatever decision he makes will be his alone. When we make decisions, we must make them with wisdom and care. The place where we find answers may not truly be the right place. The only place to find answers to the things pertaining to God is the Bible.

The Word of God is the only true basis that we have for answers concerning man's destiny or God's character. It is the one source that has endured both time and testing. If there is one untruth in the Word of God, you might well throw the whole book away. If there is one untruth, then could it be possible there is another one, and if so, which one and where?

The Trinity pertains to God, but it also has much to do with man. In order to paint a picture of the Trinity, many have resorted to analogies. Still, they represent man's futile attempt to explain the Trinity.

Chapter 3

Man—Image of God

In The Beginning:

The book of Genesis is an introduction to the first activities on earth. This is when life began its pioneering journey. When every venture became a new experience and every obstacle became a new challenge. Nevertheless, man was able to adapt to his primitive lifestyle in virtually every situation. Although nearly extinct at one point, he quickly replenished himself back into the picture. Man has endured over the years, and the legacy of his durability and triumphs are recorded in the pages of history as well as in the pages of Scripture.

Sometimes called the book of beginnings, Genesis is the first book of the Bible. Here we find the beginning of mankind, the introduction of the family, the origin of sin, the initiation of man's redemption, and the place where God first called out a people for Himself. Genesis is also the book where we want to begin our investigation into the study of the Trinity.

Creating a Profile:

For our first task, we shall examine the structure and features of man. Later we will analyze these features and evaluate what similarities they have to the Godhead. Using the Biblical account of the creation of man, will help us establish a profile to initiate this portion of our study. Our research at this point begins with the first three chapters of Genesis.

1. The First Chapter of Genesis:

The first chapter of Genesis discusses the entire creation of the heavens and the earth. We are told that God spoke the heavens and the earth, as well as everything in the heavens and the earth into existence in six days. Thus, it was on the fifth day that God made all the fowl of the air and the living creatures of the sea. Furthermore, on the sixth day He made all the cattle, creeping things and beasts of the earth. There was one other item we might mention. Also on that sixth day God made man, and that is where we want to focus our study at this point.

- And God said, Let Us make man in Our image, after Our likeness: and let them have dominion over the fish of the sea, and over the fowl of the air, and over the cattle, and over all the earth, and over every creeping thing that creepeth upon the earth. - (Genesis 1:26)

This is the first mention of man in the Scriptures, but this one verse speaks volumes concerning man's importance in life. He received authority over everything else, but more significantly, he is made in the image and likeness of God.

2. The Second Chapter of Genesis:

Looking now to the second chapter of Genesis, again we see the creation of man, but this time in more detail. Verse number seven is an interesting passage of Scripture. The entire verse contains 27 words describing how God made man.

- And the Lord God formed man of the dust of the ground, and breathed into his nostrils the breath of life; and man became a living soul. - (Genesis 2:7)

Even though there are only 27 words, this verse also contains a multitude of information. Let's take a closer look at these 27 words to see just what they do and do not tell us.

Here are some things the verse does tell us:
1. It was God who formed man.
2. God shaped or formed man out of dust from the ground.
3. God breathed into his nostrils the breath of life.
4. When God breathed into the man's nostrils he became a living soul.

Here are some things the verse did not tell us:
1. The dust had to change its makeup from dust to flesh, bone and blood.
2. The form made out of dust had to begin breathing and taking in air.
3. His heart began pumping blood throughout the body.
4. The man had to begin to think, see, feel, stand, walk, smell, hear and talk.

Man Became a Living Soul:

Now, let's review both lists in more detail. We discover that God formed man of the dust of the ground, but the form of dust was void of life until God breathed into his nostrils. At that point, the dust of the ground transformed into the fleshly part of man. Accordingly, the breath of life God breathed into man was the invisible and immaterial part of man that made him a living soul. Therefore, the dust became the flesh, and the breath of God produced the living soul.

As Adam Encountered Life:

Adam was full of life and ready to experience his assignment as the first human being. His heart began pumping pure blood throughout the body. His eyes could see, he could hear and do all the other things expected of the body. He could think, have feelings and do all the things expected of the mind and soul. Adam's whole body was operating perfectly and was full of life. Designed to live forever, it was free of disease, infection and deterioration in all of its parts.

The 27 Words:
After close examination, it becomes noteworthy to say many things took place within those 27 words. Some of the things were obvious because the verse says so; still other things were obvious because we know how the various parts of the body should perform.

Two Important Passages:
There are two more passages of Scripture we want to touch on before continuing. These passages contain some information necessary to help understand what takes place in the third chapter of Genesis. We find our first passage of importance in Genesis 2:16,17, which describes the warning about the forbidden fruit. The second passage is found in Genesis 2:21,22 and relates to how the first woman was made.

- And the Lord God commanded the man, saying, Of every tree of the garden thou mayest freely eat: - (Genesis 2:16)
- But of the tree of the knowledge of good and evil, thou shalt not eat of it: for in the day that thou eatest thereof thou shalt surely die. - (Genesis 2:17)

- And the LORD God caused a deep sleep to fall upon Adam, and he slept: and He took one of his ribs, and closed up the flesh instead thereof - (Genesis 2:21)
- And the rib, which the LORD God had taken from man, made He a woman, and brought her unto the man. - (Genesis 2:22)

Up to this point, God created man in His own image and likeness. He told man to replenish and subdue the earth and granted to man the dominion authority over all the earth. Recorded in Genesis 2:16,17, Adam received a commandment given to him by God, while Genesis 2:21,22 reveals that the woman is actually a by-product of the man.

3. The Third Chapter of Genesis:

As we look ahead at the third chapter, we find that the serpent deceived the woman, and she ate of the forbidden fruit from the tree of the knowledge of good and evil.

- And the serpent said unto the woman, Ye shall not surely die - (Genesis 3:4)
- For God doth know that in the day that ye eat thereof, then your eyes shall be opened, and ye shall be as gods, knowing good and evil. - (Genesis 3:5)
- And when the woman saw that the tree *was* good for food, and that it *was* pleasant to the eyes, and a tree to be desired to make *one* wise, she took of the fruit thereof, and did eat, and gave also unto her husband with her; and he did eat. - (Genesis 3:6)

These Scriptures are commonly referred to as "the fall of man." This is where death first occurred in man. Chapter three also reveals the results of the fall of man and includes the following:

1. The man and woman became aware they were naked, and God knew they had sinned.
2. God told the serpent that He would put enmity between the seed of the serpent and the seed of the woman.
3. Because of sin, the fleshly part of man began a process whereby it would eventually die and go back to the dust from whence it came.
4. The man and woman both received a curse, and God banished them from the "Garden of Eden."

The Result of Disobedience:

As it turned out, man became separated from God because of his disobedience. The result of this separation created a void within man; a void that only God can fill. As it is, man must now find a way back to God, his only hope.

All humanity inherited the knowledge of good and evil from Adam. Consequently, all humanity also became accountable for that knowledge along with its responsibilities.

Interestingly, the physical part of man did not die immediately because we find that Adam had sons and daughters, including Cain and Abel. Adam died at the age of 930 years. Although God banished them from the garden, He still permitted them to replenish the earth. If Adam and Eve had died immediately after the fall, there would be no procreation, and thus no more man. However, God did not want the creation that He produced just to fall by the wayside, so He allowed man the time to produce children. In this way, the plan He purposed from the beginning would develop just as He established it to happen.

No Children Before the Fall:
Another thing to keep in mind is this—there were no children born to Adam and Eve before the fall. Why is this important? Because a child who was born before the fall would have inherited Adam's sinless nature. Under these circumstances, there could have been sinless individuals available to produce other sinless human beings. The sinless offspring would retain all the characteristics of Adam before the fall of man.

Although the offspring of Adam would inherit death because of his disobedience, the offspring of the sinless children would not be under that curse. That is, unless they also sinned. In that case, they, and any offspring produced by them, would come under the same curse of death as Adam and his descendants.

God's True Concern and the Situation:
One important factor to consider here: The creation was not God's total concern. He has a great love for man and a great desire for his fellowship. He loves man even more than we can imagine. Man is the only creature that God created in His own

image and likeness. He wanted to share His Kingdom with someone like Himself. However, in the midst of creating a being like man, He also created another situation.

For man to love God in return, it was essential for man to have a *free will*. That was the only way it could be. If man did not have a *free will*, he would be as a robot, unable to make his own decisions, and forced to love God and obey His commandments. With a *free will*, man can choose to accept God's love and fellowship, or reject them. The choice is solely up to the man to make—God cannot make the choice for him.

In Summary of Chapter Three:

The first chapter of Genesis was an informative outline of man. Often it's not what the Scriptures say, but what they do not say that enable us to gather large quantities of information. Such is the case where God breathed the breath of life into man's nostrils. Man became a living soul, but there was no mention regarding his bodily functions. By sorting through bits and pieces of information, we were able create a profile to add credence to what really happened at the creation of mankind.

The third chapter of Genesis records the fall of man. Being deceived by the serpent, the woman ate of the forbidden fruit and gave it to Adam; he also ate. Because of man's disobedience, God banished them from the "Garden of Eden." However, another result of the disobedience was that all of mankind received the consequence of sin.

Obviously, there was more that occurred in the "Garden" than we can comprehend. All the same, we are able to gain much insight through careful study of the Scriptures. The fallout that developed from this dreadful event still haunts man to this day. However, good news arose from the aftermath, and that is the central theme of why and how the Trinity came into being.

Chapter 4

The Make-up of Man

Examining Spiritual Issues:
Next, we want to examine the features of man, namely th
body, soul and spirit. Issues relating to spiritual matters remai
a gray area, and one by which we are unable to probe except b
the Word of God. Fortunately, there are many Scriptur
passages relevant to each component of man. Given the benefi
of these Scriptures, we are able to receive considerable insigh
regarding the specifics that constitute man.

Earlier we examined one such Scripture in the second chapte
of Genesis. We found that several things happened when Go
breathed the breath of life into the nostrils of man. It must b
pointed out that something else also occurred at that time
Besides becoming a living soul, the Spirit of God entered int
man. To obtain a better understanding of this, let's take a loo
at three passages from the book of Job:

- As God liveth, who hath taken away my judgment; and th
  Almighty, who hath vexed my soul; all the while my breat
  is in me, and the Spirit of God is in my nostrils; my lip
  shall not speak wickedness, nor my tongue utter deceit.
  (Job 27:2-4)

- The Spirit of God hath made me, and the breath of th
  Almighty hath given me life. - (Job 33:4)

- If He set His heart upon man, *if* He gather unto Himself His Spirit and His breath; all flesh shall perish together, and man shall turn again unto dust. - (Job 34:14,15)

Notice from these three passages of Job that the Spirit of God is in man. Job 27:2-4 indicates that the Spirit of God is in the nostrils of Job. The second passage, Job 33:4, restates the breath of God giving life. The last verse declares: If God would ever take back His Spirit and His breath from mankind, all flesh would perish. Hence, when God breathed into man, not only His breath, but also His Spirit entered into man and we can conclude that all humanity is kept alive by these two essentials.

The Totality of Man:
The body, soul and spirit are the three components that contain the totality of man, and they are the very particulars we want to expound upon in this chapter. Obviously, the fleshly part of man is the essential quality that we can see and touch, whereas the soul and spirit are invisible to our physical senses.

The Only Scripture:
Only one Scripture passage mentions the body, soul, and spirit together. In the lone passage from 1 Thessalonians, we find the apostle Paul exhorting the brethren at Thessalonica:

- And the very God of peace sanctify you wholly; and *I pray God* your whole spirit and soul and body be preserved blameless unto the coming of our Lord Jesus Christ. - (1 Thessalonians 5:23)

Let's look at one other Scripture verse grouping the body, soul and spirit together. This passage is found in the book of Hebrews. In this verse, the soul and spirit are presented together, but the body is represented by a different set of features, namely the joints and marrow:

- For the Word of God *is* quick, and powerful, and sharper than any two-edged sword, piercing even to the dividing asunder of soul and spirit, and of the joints and marrow, and *is* a discerner of the thoughts and intents of the heart. - (Hebrews 4:12)

A View of Man's Composition:
We can define the body (flesh) as the physical house for the soul and the spirit. The body is also that element designed for recognition and performing essential work while on earth.

In contrast, the soul is *the life force* of man and his inner life. It contains the nucleus of his thoughts and emotions and is the controlling force of the body. God made man a living soul; therefore, the soul is not only the eternal part of man, but also the spiritual component made in the image of God. The dwelling place for the soul is within the body for as long as the individual remains on earth.

Forasmuch as the soul is *the life force*, the spirit is *the life source* and is considered as the heart and focus of man's affections and desires. We also find that the spirit is God's dwelling place in man and the conduit whereby the Spirit of God (*The Life Source*) flows into man.

Spiritual Death:
The events that transpired in the "Garden of Eden," resulted in separation from God. Before the fall, Adam was mindful of only good and the Spirit of God filled his heart. After the fall, Adam's heart inherited the knowledge of good and evil. By disobeying God's warning, sin entered the heart of man causing a separation of the Spirit of God from the spirit of man. This separation resulted in a void on the inside of man and is referred to as spiritual death. So, with the Spirit of God absent from the spirit of Adam, the result was spiritual death.

Without *The Life Source* (the Spirit of God) to sustain him, Adam gradually died. His physical body died at the age of 930 years; however, the soul of Adam also lacked the regenerating life of God's Spirit. Consequently, when Adam died bodily, the eternal living soul went to the place of the dead. "For as the body without the spirit is dead..." James 2:26. Still, even though the body is dead, the soul remains functional and aware of its surroundings, but without God, it has no life.

At this point, let us take a closer look at the three facets of man's individuality from a biblical viewpoint, beginning with the body, then the soul, and in conclusion, the spirit.

1. The Bodily Attribute of Man:

The make-up of the body is familiar to us and for that reason, we shall discuss only the details necessary for our study. The body is that part of man that is visible and touchable, in contrast to the soul and spirit. It is the means of physical identification and interacting with others while on earth. It also provides a dwelling place for the seat of sensations and data supplied by the five senses. Essentially, flesh, blood and bone make up the composition of the body. The Bible informs us that the blood gives life to the flesh.

- For the life of the flesh *is* in the blood: and I have given it to you upon the altar to make an atonement for your souls: for it *is* the blood *that* maketh an atonement for the soul. - (Leviticus 17:11)

This passage uncovers two vital things about the blood. First the flesh gets its life from the blood. We find that this blood originated with the first man (Adam). "And (God) hath made of one blood all nations of men for to dwell on the face of the earth, and hath determined the times before appointed, and the bounds of their habitation..." Acts 17:26.

The blood of the first man was so pure that there was no impurity or contamination anywhere in its composition. Nevertheless, the blood of Adam became polluted when he disobeyed God, and essentially all humanity became infected

The second thing determined from the verse in Leviticus is that blood was designed for making atonement for the soul. This was a channel to draw man back to God by providing reconciliation for sin. Habakkuk 1:13 discloses, "Thou art of purer eyes than to behold evil, and canst not look on iniquity...." God cannot look on iniquity, but if covered by the blood sacrifice to atone for sin, God can look upon the sin, but all He notices is the blood.

In the Old Testament, the high priest went into the tabernacle to sprinkle blood on the altar and other places. Although it was essential that animals selected for the sacrifices be without spot or blemish, their blood was not a perfect sacrifice. In view of that, the high priest performed this ceremony every year. The Old Testament atonement was actually only a shadow of the blood shed once and for all by Jesus. He became the sinless, spotless sacrifice required by God for the atonement.

The heart is the very core of the physical body and pumps the life-giving blood to every part of the body. Once the heart stops beating, the blood flow ceases and death occurs. At the point where physical death takes place, the soul begins its journey in life alone.

2. The Soul of Man:
The soul is the immaterial and immortal part of man. Expressed as the conscious center of thoughts and emotions, the soul is also identified as the natural man and focus of man's personality. This is the part of man that goes on after the death of the physical body.

As the life of the flesh is in the blood, the life of the soul comes from the spirit of man. The soul is also the element made after the image and likeness of God. The following Scriptures will lend an awareness regarding the design and destiny of the soul:

- But his flesh upon him shall have pain, and his soul within him shall mourn. - (Job 14:22)

His flesh has the pain but the soul mourns. This verse also shows that the soul is within the body.

- And they said one to another, We *are* verily guilty concerning our brother, in that we saw the anguish of his soul, when he besought us, and we would not hear; therefore is this distress come upon us. - (Genesis 42:21)

To see the anguish created by the soul of their brother indicates that while the soul is the immaterial and immortal part; whatsoever the soul does, the flesh does likewise. Thus, their brother's emotions trickled through from the soul to the flesh.

- And he stretched himself upon the child three times, and cried unto the Lord, and said, O Lord my God, I pray Thee, let this child's soul come into him again. - (1 Kings 17:21)
- And the Lord heard the voice of Elijah; and the soul of the child came into him again, and he revived. - (1 Kings 17:22)

This passage signifies that the child's soul departed out from his physical body. Then again, it was the soul that came back into the child and revived his physical body. This also clarifies the soul departing the body at death.

- Therefore I will not refrain my mouth; I will speak in the anguish of my spirit; I will complain in the bitterness of my soul. - (Job 7:11)

In this verse from Job 7:11, we find all three features that shape the structure of man presented in one verse. "I will not refrain my mouth" symbolizes the body. Job is saying that he will not quit talking in the suffering of his spirit, even though his soul is bitter. This illustrates again the emotions displayed by the soul.

- And fear not them which kill the body, but are not able to kill the soul: but rather fear Him which is able to destroy both soul and body in hell. - (Matthew 10:28)

This verse from Matthew's gospel, proclaims the ability to kill the body, but not the soul. It verifies the soul as the eternal part of man and that the soul lives on after the death of an individual. This passage of Scripture also points out that we are not to fear man, for he cannot kill the real individual living inside the body, but rather fear God.

- And thou shalt love the Lord thy God with all thy heart, and with all thy soul, and with all thy mind, and with all thy strength: this is the first commandment. - (Mark 12:30)

Here we see the relationship of the soul to the center of the thoughts and emotions. Illustrated in this verse are the similarities between the make-up of man and the individuality of the Trinity. Although the body, soul and spirit of man have different functions, they still add up to one man. Likewise, the Father, Son and Holy Spirit in similar fashion, have different functions, but still add up to one God.

- For what is a man profited, if he shall gain the whole world, and lose his own soul? or what shall a man give in exchange for his soul? - (Matthew 16:26)

This passage illustrates the worth of the soul along with the fact that an individual's soul belongs solely to the individual.

3. The Spirit Part of Man:

The Hebrew word for spirit is Ruah. The Greek word is Pneuma. Both words mean to blow, breathe or spirit. The spirit of man is the controlling influence and the focal point of his affections. In addition, it is referred to as the life principle infused into man by God and the part of man that connects to God. Not only that, but the spirit of man functions as the component desiring to worship and serve God. As the soul receives its life from the spirit of man, the spirit of man receives its life from the Spirit of God. The following are Scriptures with references to the spirit of man:

- And Hannah answered and said, No, my lord, I *am* a woman of a sorrowful spirit: I have drunk neither wine nor strong drink, but have poured out my soul before the Lord. - (1 Samuel 1:15)

Here, we see the feelings of Hannah coming out, as she describes herself as a woman whose spirit is sorrowful because she was childless. At the end of this verse, the soul is being described as Hannah pours out her emotions, full of sorrow because she could not have a child.

- Then shall the dust return to the earth as it was: and the spirit shall return unto God who gave it.- (Ecclesiastes 12:7)

This particular verse of Scripture grants us a view of what happens to the spirit of man at death.

- I Daniel was grieved in my spirit in the midst of *my* body... - (Daniel 7:15)

This verse clearly illustrates that the spirit is within the midst of the body, commonly referred to as the heart of a person.

- The spirit of man *is* the candle of the LORD, searching all the inward parts of the belly. - (Proverbs 20:27)

In this verse we find a different use for the spirit of man. God is able to disclose much about our true motives through our spirit. It indicates how God is capable of distinguishing man's attitude toward Him and the individual's desire for salvation.

- Watch and pray, that ye enter not into temptation: the spirit indeed *is* willing, but the flesh *is* weak. - (Matthew 26:41)

Jesus spoke these words to His disciples in the *Garden of Gethsemane* and we find kinship of the spirit with the heart. Consequently, the spirit (heart) desired to watch and pray, but the flesh was weak and in this case, sleep overtook them.

- The Spirit itself beareth witness with our spirit, that we are the children of God: - (Romans 8:16)

Here we find the Holy Spirit is referred to as the Spirit, bearing witness with our spirit. Life is touching life, as the heart of God unites with the heart of man. The feelings, motivations, and thoughts of man confirm his relationship with God.

- The burden of the word of the LORD for Israel, saith the LORD, which stretcheth forth the heavens, and layeth the foundation of the earth, and formeth the spirit of man within him. - (Zechariah 12:1)

Here we have verification of the spirit of man. Why is this important? The fact is, when God breathed into man's nostrils, there was no disclosure of man having a spirit. The first mention of the spirit of man does not occur until the 41st chapter of Genesis. This also helps show how it is possible with the help of other Scriptures, to fill in details of the creation.

An Illustration of Spiritual Death:

We mentioned spiritual death earlier in this chapter—now let's take a closer look at how this occurred. Man's spirit was originally in union with God's Spirit while he was in the "Garden of Eden." The harmony between God and man became estranged at the instant of man's disobedience. Only when Adam disobeyed God's command did he obtain the knowledge of good and evil. Then was his eyes open, and they both knew they were naked. It was the sin that produced spiritual death in man, not the knowledge of good and evil. After they sinned, they acquired the knowledge. To illustrate what transpired at the time of this spiritual death, let's consider the following:

The Wire and the Switch: The Power Company sends electricity into our homes by way of electric wires. These wires connect to wires laced throughout the home. The electricity in the wires provides power to lights and receptacles controlled by switches. If the light switch is in the "off" position, the power is still available at the top of the switch. Nevertheless, the light will not light until the switch is in the "on" position.

Likewise, we want to picture Adam being formed from the dust of the ground. Imagine a certain length of electrical wire placed inside him from his head to his heart (spirit). Again, envision in the middle of this wire—a switch. At the very creation of man the switch was in the "on" position. When God breathed the breath of life into man's nostrils, the Spirit of God surged through the wire and the switch into the heart of man. The spirit of man was in direct contact with the Spirit of God. The power radiated by the Spirit of God brought Life into the spirit of man, which in turn, released life into man's soul.

In contrast—at the fall, and even to this day, that switch is in the "off" position because of disobedience to God's command. In spite of this, the Spirit of God resides in the head part of man, but cannot reach the heart because the switch remains in the "off" position.

We must make one thing clear. Although we used the term "spiritual death," it was not the spirit of man that died; it was the soul. The spirit is that part that belongs to God and returns to Him at death. The soul is the real person living inside the body and belongs to each individual. It will follow him eternally to the place that he determines on earth as the place where he wants to spend eternity after his physical death.

Man is Unable to Free Himself:

The consequences caused by man's disobedience is without recourse. The sentence of death continues without expectation of parole. Man is helpless to work his way free, and no matter how good he tries to be, he is powerless to free himself. Sin cannot enter into heaven. God cannot look upon iniquity, and neither can He look upon the contaminated blood of man.

Nothing man attempts to do will free him from this predicament. Jesus said, "It is the spirit that quickeneth; the flesh profiteth nothing..." John 6:63.

Life is in the spirit, but only when that spirit is connected to God's Spirit. Just as man's disobedience brought about spiritual death, so also man's obedience to Satan's deception brought man under Satan's rule and ultimately he obtained Satan's fate.

Man Was Made in God's Image:

The Scripture passages relating to the body, soul and spirit of man were randomly selected. There were many other related passages we could have acknowledged, but these will give us a reasonable view of the whole man. Along these lines, and from this framework, we want to gather a little more insight into the similarities of God and man.

To harvest this information, it would be worthwhile to have another look at a passage of Scripture we met earlier. By turning our attention to Genesis 1:26, we find the place where God said, "...let Us make man in Our image, after Our likeness...." Interestingly, this part of the verse suggests that God is talking to someone. As a consequence, by using the words Us and Our, it suggests He was talking to Himself since there is only one God. Taking a look at Genesis 1:2 we find where the Spirit of God moved upon the face of the waters. Could it be God was talking to his own Spirit? That seems to be the only conclusion we can reach.

Because the Spirit of God was mentioned could it be possible God also has a Soul? The following Scriptures reveal the answer:

- And I will set My tabernacle among you: and **My Soul** shall not abhor you. And I will walk among you, and will be your God, and ye shall be My people. - (Leviticus 26:11,12)

- Your new moons and your appointed feast **My Soul** hateth: they are a trouble unto Me; I am weary to bear *them*. - (Isaiah 1:14)

- Behold My Servant, whom I uphold; Mine Elect, in whom **My Soul** delighteth; I have put My Spirit upon Him: He shall bring forth judgment to the Gentiles. - (Isaiah 42:1)

Also see Jeremiah 6:8 and 9:9. These Scriptures illustrate how God has two of the three entities that also make up man, namely, the Spirit and the Soul. What about the Body? As we shall see in a later chapter, there is indeed a Body included within the Godhead. For now, here are some of the vital points covered in this chapter that will be of significance later.

Summary Chapter Four:

In our exploration of the body, soul and spirit, we uncovered valuable data regarding their application and design. The body is essentially the tent that houses the soul and spirit of man. The life of the flesh is in the blood. Another use for the blood is the atonement for sin. The soul is the force of life, and seat of the thoughts and emotions. It is the part of a person made in the image and likeness of God. The spirit is the source of life and control center for the affections. The spirit of man is also the channel whereby he receives life from the Spirit of God.

We were able to display how some aspects of the body, soul and spirit actually fit in with man's eternal destiny. For instance, we have determined that at death, the body returns to the dust of the ground. The soul goes to the place determined by the choice of the individual while on earth. The spirit goes back to God who gave it.

Before the fall, God and man united spiritually one with another. After the fall, man became spiritually separated from God. The wire and the switch illustrated this idea. Man retained a head knowledge of God, but no longer a heart knowledge. This created a void within the heart of man. Without God's Spirit living in the heart of man, spiritual death occurred.

Spiritually speaking, when we take into account the outer-man (the body) with respect to the inner-man (the soul), man cannot change on the outside until a change is made on the inside.

When comparing the characteristics of God to that of man, we find that God has a Spirit and a Soul. The question remains; does God also have a Body? The answer is "yes," as we shall discover in later chapters.

Chapter 5

Trinity and Religion

Religion and Reasons:

Man's natural instinct is to seek after a way to satisfy his spiritual hunger. He senses a void in his life but is unable to reason what or why. Without God's Spirit to fill man's spirit with life, he impulsively searches for anything with a spiritual tone to it. If it impresses him, he will usually follow it, sometimes without wise judgment. More often than not, religion is the way he chooses to fill the spiritual void. The bad news is—there are many paths available for him to travel, each claiming to be the right one. The book of Proverbs tells us:

- There is a way that seemeth right unto a man, but the end thereof *are* the ways of death. - (Proverbs 14:12)

Religion is essentially a belief in a Supreme Being, any being, a thing, a makeup of the universe, or a philosophy. Things considered sacred vary from religion to religion, but include the sun, moon, stars, animals, statues, buildings, gods, and goddesses. Usually incorporated into the belief system is some form of prayer, worship, or ceremony and a religious leader who is employed to conduct the designated ceremonies. Moreover, most religions include documented sets of rules, or guidelines, for their members to abide by. Monotheism is the term used for the worship of one God, while polytheism is the worship of more than one god.

In this chapter we have selected eight non-Christian world religions, which represent a broad assortment of cultures and beliefs. The first four religions for our review are Buddhism, Hinduism, Islam and Judaism, while the last four include Confucianism, Taoism, Bahaism and Shinto. This evaluation will provide a better perception of what various non-Christian religions advise their followers regarding the Trinity.

Beliefs of Non-Christian Religions:
Buddhism: Founded around 525 B.C. in northern India by a man, known as Gautama Siddhartha, also recognized as the Buddha (*enlightened one*). The sacred text, called the Tripitaka, contains the collection of Buddha's teachings and doctrines centered on "*The Three Jewels*":
1. The dharma (the sacred teachings of Buddha),
2. The sangha (the community of followers that now includes nuns, monks, and laity),
3. Refuge in Buddha.

Buddhism is widely found among Asian nations where temples and shrine dedicated to Buddha were built. Ceremonies include meditation, chanting, temple rites, and exorcism. Buddhism is a religion devoid of authority. Each follower of Buddha is accountable for his or her actions and responsible for whatever he or she does. Buddha became enlightened as to ways of combating personal desires. These precepts, called the "*Four Noble Truths*," have become the substance of Buddhism.

The following discloses the theme of the "*Four Noble Truths*":
(1) Life is suffering,
(2) Desires and ignorance of reality cause all suffering,
(3) Overcoming desires and ignorance of reality can end suffering,
(4) The path to eradicating the suffering is "*The Eightfold Path*."

"*The Eightfold Path*" consists of: (1) right belief, (2) right intention, (3) right speech, (4) right action, (5) right livelihood, (6) right effort, (7) right thought, (8) right contemplation.

Sometimes called the eight steps to salvation in Buddhism, "*The Eightfold Path*" does *not* contain ways to get into heaven. Instead, it includes ideas designed to keep one from worldly attachments, and keeping all rules and regulations, which help break the cycle of death. This in turn achieves freedom from pain and suffering. This does not mean annihilation, but an extinction of passions and desires, resulting in absolute purity.

Council meetings formed after Buddha's death to compile his teachings and disciplinary guidelines. Over the years several different schools of Buddhist thought have resulted in the formation of various texts. The two main strands of Buddhism (*Theravada and Mahayana*) are predominant in Eastern culture, while *Zen Buddhism* has gained interest in the Western world.

Even though Buddhism seems unchallenging, barriers of the religion exist when considering some of the areas involved in achieving well-being and perfection. By following the guidelines set forth in Buddha's teachings, the religion of Buddhism looks inward to self to achieve its goals. Heaven, hell, sin, man's soul, and other items of importance to other religions do not hold much credence here. That brings us to the question—what about the Trinity?

God - Buddhism does not recognize a God or Supreme Being. God is not a Creator, nor does He control human destiny. Some Buddhists think of Buddha as a god or an enlightened being, although Buddhism exists mainly from an atheistic viewpoint.
Jesus - Some may consider Jesus an enlightened man, but He has no place in Buddhism's theology.
Holy Spirit - He is not a part of Buddhism's system of belief.

Hinduism: Hinduism, which is the primary religion in India, is also the world's oldest religion. Hinduism is rapidly increasing in interest around the world as there are over 800,000 followers of the Hindu religion worldwide. Hinduism has no particular founder and exactly when it first began is unknown, perhaps as early as 4000 B.C. The significant meaning of the word Hindu is river or ocean.

The religion does not adhere to a specified set of doctrines although there are certain principles incorporated into the belief system. Special ancient writings, called *Vedas*, meaning knowledge, are for guidance purposes. These writings also contain prayers and hymns used to worship gods.

Considered sacred to the Hindus are cows, monkeys, snakes and other animals. Pilgrimages include those to Benares on the Ganges River in India. Among Hindu ceremonies are ones focusing on birth, marriage and death.

Reincarnation plays a major part in the religion as does a concept called *karma*. The law of *karma* concerns the moral character of a pre-existence to determine the level of existence in the new life. They also believe in *Brahmanism*—the supreme essence of the universe whereby all divinity forms subsist. Deities dwell in Hindu temples where they receive offerings. Yoga is another practice of the Hindu religion.

The religion is strictly polytheistic, meaning a belief in the existence of many gods, or divine beings. As a result, dissimilarities exist in the principles used in devotions and in the specific beliefs of an individual follower. Within the substantial assortment of gods to be found in Hinduism, there exists a structure similar to the Trinity—Brahma the Godhead or Creator, Vishnu the Preserver and Shiva the Destroyer.

Overall, the religion of Hinduism is unique in the fact that it has no one founder and no distinctive set of rules to follow. Because it is polytheistic, Hinduism cannot incorporate the Trinity into its theology. The following is traditionally how Hinduism views the three Persons of the Godhead.

God - Many divinity forms are part of a universal spirit called Brahman. Brahma is considered the creator of the universe.
Jesus - A guru, good teacher, a son of God, as others are. He did not rise from the dead.
Holy Ghost - Hinduism does not recognize the Holy Spirit.

Islam: Islam is one of two major non-Christian religions with a belief in one God (*monotheistic*). A man named Mohammed founded the Islamic religion in Arabia in 622 A.D. Mohammed was born in 570 A.D. at Mecca, now recognized as Islam's most Holy City. He preached that he was the messenger of the one God (*Allah*). Followers of Mohammed and his teachings, are called Muslims. Islam means surrender to the will of God.

The Islamic sacred text, called the Qur'an (*Koran*), contains the words of Allah, as delivered to Mohammed by the angel Gabriel. A mosque is the place of prayer and worship for the Muslim. The chief officer in the mosque is the Imam. His principal duty is leading the people in prayer. Rituals include akikah (*birth ceremony*), shahada (*initiation*), marriage and funeral services. Ramadan, a holy festival in the ninth month of the Islamic calendar, calls for daily repentance and fasting.

Estimates have placed the number of Islamic believers at over one billion members. Although followers of the religion are found worldwide—the Middle East, Indonesia and Northern Africa have the greatest concentration of Muslims. Disputes over leadership led to the formation of splinter groups, including these three: Shiites, Sunnites, and Wahhabi.

The primary duties of Islam, also called *the Five Pillars*, are:

1. The profession of faith: the belief and confession that there is no God but *Allah*, and the status of Mohammed as prophet.
2. Prayer: Pray five times a day toward Mecca.
3. Almsgiving: Give one fortieth of income for the needy.
4. Fasting: To fast during the month of Ramadan between sunrise and sunset.
5. The Hajj: Makes a pilgrimage to Mecca at least once in a lifetime, if possible.

The Qur'an forbids lying, stealing, adultery, and murder. Unjust killing is punishable by death, except for accidental killing, where "blood money" is paid to the surviving relatives.

Islam teaches of a heaven, hell, and judgment day. The sorrows of hell have a resemblance to those described in the Bible, but heaven to the Muslim is a garden, flowing streams, fruit, and beautiful virgins. God (*Allah*) created the universe, is omnipotent, just, and merciful. Man is God's highest creation.

Although Islam is a monotheistic religion, and the Qur'an contains some words of Jesus, Islam does not accept the Trinity within its design. The following is a general perception of the Islamic view of the Trinity.

God - Although some similarities exist, *Allah* is not the same God as worshipped by Christianity. To the Muslim, *Allah* is a strict judge, but He can also be merciful. He is just and wants man to repent and purify himself while on earth.

Jesus - He was a prophet like Abraham, Moses, Isaiah, and Mohammed, and perceived as a messenger from God in His time. Jesus is not divine or God.

Holy Spirit - In the Qur'an, Jesus is referred to as the Spirit of God. The angel Gabriel is the same as the Holy Spirit.

Judaism: This religion began around 1900 B.C. when God made a covenant with the patriarch, Abraham. The covenant passed down to Abraham's son, Isaac, and his grandson, Jacob, also called Israel. The Hebrew Bible, specifically the five books of Moses, known as the *Torah*, contain the references to the covenant. It represents the religious structure of Judaism and the heritage of the Jewish people. The covenant discloses that Abraham would become the father of a great nation and God would bless all the nations through him.

Within the *Torah*, "The Ten Commandments" and the basic laws of Judaism are found. The Hebrew Bible is the same as Christianity's Old Testament. In contrast, Judaism does not regard the New Testament as part of its teachings. The religion of Judaism relates exclusively to the Jewish people. Jews are found worldwide, but they claim Israel as their homeland and Jerusalem as their most holy city.

The Hebrew Bible not only foretold the dispersion of Israel into the nations, but also that they would return again to their homeland. This occurred in 1948 when the United Nations agreed to grant Palestine as the homeland for the Jews. The city of Jerusalem, in Israel, is the place where the most holy site, the Temple, stood until the Romans destroyed it in 70 A.D.

Judaism's place of worship is the synagogue. A Rabbi serves as spiritual leader. Circumcision, performed on Jewish boys at the age of eight days old, is the symbol of the covenant God made with Abraham. At thirteen years of age the Jewish boy receives his *bar mitzvah*, making him a full member of the Jewish community. Judaism consists of three religious groups: the Orthodox, the Reform and the Conservative. Of the three, the Orthodox maintains the strictest adherence in observing Jewish laws and traditions.

During World War II, more than six million Jews were put to death because of the Holocaust. Today there are nearly 17 million Jews who hold to the beliefs of Judaism. It is the oldest religion to teach monotheism or the existence of one God. The Jews believe that one day a Messiah will come to redeem humanity. The Messiah will be a descendent from the house of David. Judaism does not recognize the Trinity. Some believe the Trinity teaches three Gods instead of one. The following reflects how Judaism projects the Trinity within its teachings.

God - The Almighty Creator and Absolute Ruler. God is a Spiritual Being. He is to be worshipped and obeyed. God is merciful and just. The God of Judaism is the same God as worshipped by Christians.

Jesus - To some He is a false Messiah, to others He is a good man and teacher. He is not God or the Messiah.

Holy Spirit - God's love and power expressed on the earth.

Other Non-Christian Religions:

Confucianism: Confucius (551-479 B.C.) was born in northern China. He was a brilliant teacher who viewed education not as learning and accumulating knowledge, but as a means of self-transformation. Before Confucius was three, his father died, leaving his impoverished mother to raise the child alone. Discipline and preparation paid off as his academic studies were above average. In his twenties he held several government positions; yet, after a brief marriage, he went on to become a tutor. He soon attracted a circle of devoted disciples as well as a growing reputation for his ingenious theories and ideas.

After his death, a number of followers compiled the deeds and sayings of Confucius. They put his accomplishments into a collection called the *Anolects*. A notable theory of Confucius was that for an individual's righteousness to exist, importance must reside in the virtuous conduct of the state ruler.

The cultivation of virtues is central to Confucianism's teachings. Two primary virtues are *jen*: a compassionate and humanitarian attitude, and *li*: proper behavior and ritualistic conduct to enhance the life of the individual, his family, and the state. Confucianism stresses moral conduct and right relationships rather than religious convictions or spiritual efforts. Considered a religion by many, the convictions and theories of Confucianism closely resemble that of a philosophy. It attempts to establish ethical standards and promote virtuous conduct among rulers. In so doing, moral standards and right relationships will emerge.

Over the centuries Confucianism generated new schools of thought, thereby enhancing the theories and ideas presented by Confucius. Although his teachings have diminished somewhat in the 20th century, the standards and traditions continue to be part of the culture of China and other East Asian countries. This religion has no ties whatsoever to the Trinity.

God - No God or gods are observed.
Jesus - No opinion expressed.
Holy Spirit - No opinion expressed.

Taoism: Taoism became a major religion of China around the 4th century B.C. The writings of *Lao-Tzu*, dating about the 3rd century B.C., are the important text from which Taoism originates. Tao means "path" or "way." The basic doctrines are compassion, moderation and humility. Through these doctrines, Taoism seeks to inoculate the individual with the following virtues: goodness, simplicity, gentleness and purity.

Many ideas of Buddhism also influenced the Taoist religion as it adopted temple worship and organized monastery orders. Several sects have risen from Taoism; however, each sect is established on the original philosophy of the religion.

Some groups involve faith healings, exorcisms, and meditation. The principle of Taoism is primarily an attitude toward life, but one objective is to achieve unity with the Tao and the mystical powers it contains. Tao is attained when the individual empties himself of all doctrines and knowledge. The powers formulate into longevity and immortality when assisted by meditation, breathing exercises, medicinal plants and magical remedies.

In our present day, the government of China has tried to suppress Taoism. Despite that, the religion continues in mainline China, Taiwan, Hong Kong, and to some extent, in Western culture. Through the practices of acupuncture and martial arts as a means to achieve physical well being, Westerners have come to embrace these features as beneficial. As far as spiritual implications are concerned—the religion offers no remedy to restore man back to God. Moreover, it also fails to deal with the sinful nature of man. Taoism pays no homage whatsoever to the God of the Trinity.

God - Lao-Tzu was deified and worshipped by some.
Jesus - Not a part of Taoism.
Holy Spirit - Not a part of Taoism.

Bahaism: Founded in Persia in 1863 A.D. by Mirza Husayn Ali, a man also known as Bahaullah (1817-1892). Bahaism emerged as a religion by expanding the teachings of Mirza Ali Muhammad of Shiraz (1819-1850), also known as *the Bab*. In 1844, *the Bab* foretold that a prophet would come of the progression of Abraham, Moses, Buddha, Jesus and Mohammed. In 1863, Bahaullah proclaimed himself to be that prophet. *The Bab's* teachings focused mainly on a universal society. The faith principles of Bahaullah's writings are ideas based on unity of one religion and one government. Other standards included in Bahaullah's writings are sexual equality, and the elimination of religious and racial prejudice.

Bahaism has expanded into over 300 countries, with an estimated following of over 5.5 million Bahais worldwide. The headquarters for Baha'i Faith is in Israel, with a shrine to *the Bab* located on Mount Carmel where it overlooks the cities of Haifa and Akko. The principal foundation for the religion of Baha'i Faith is established mainly upon knowing and living the teachings of Bahaullah and doing good works.

God - Revealed through Bahaullah and other religious leaders who preceded him, including Abraham, Moses, Buddha, Jesus and Mohammed.

Jesus - Is not God, but is one of the expressions of God. Did not rise from the dead.

Holy Spirit - The divine energy of God.

Shintoism: This Japanese religion dates back to prehistoric times and came into being without a name or dogma. In the 6th century A.D., Shintoism received its name in order to distinguish it from Buddhism and Confucianism. Soon after the introduction of Buddhism into Japanese culture, that religion gradually overshadowed Shintoism.

In the 1700s Shinto devotees ventured to distinguish and revitalize the traditions of the past. This succeeded in the 1800s when Shinto rites formally dissociated from Buddhist practices. Today's Shinto has integrated into Japanese customs and initiatives and is nearly indistinguishable from everyday life.

The religion is polytheistic and therefore practices the worship of many gods. Shintoists refer to this worship of many gods as *kami*. Kami is the basic force in things of nature, which includes natural bodies such as the sun, earth, trees, rivers, rocks and storms. The religion emphasizes rituals and moral standards, yet no specific dogma restricts a practitioner from expressing a belief in a particular *kami*.

Most events of faith are held in shrines. The locations of shrines are commonly centered close to sacred trees and flowing waters. Ceremonies performed by Shintoist include great purification, long life, peace, abundant harvest, and good health. Worshippers recite prayers of thanksgiving and give offerings such as cloth, cakes and flowers to the *kami*. Shintoism does not stress life after death or belief in the Trinity.

God - In Shintoism, the basic force within is called *kami*, the worship of many gods.
Jesus - Not a part of Shintoism.
Holy Spirit - Not a part of Shintoism.

Conclusion of Non-Christian Religions:

This concludes our analysis of the eight non-Christian religions. At best, we barely touched the surface relating to the extent of ideas and practices regarding each one. Listing every religion, cult, or philosophy, along with each deity, worship and teaching, could get confusing.

We must realize that religions are continually being established, and certainly more will be introduced the future. In reality, many paths exist for man to travel down on his quest for spiritual fulfillment. If one does not fulfill his need, he can always try another. Many times the individual will believe the dogma of a religion without giving much thought to the discernment of its truth. This fact is brought to light in the conflicting reports we uncover later.

Closer examination reveals that many of these religions were part of a culture that existed for centuries. In some territories, strong relationships were formed toward a particular religion and families were expected to adhere to certain beliefs. When these religious values are instilled during childhood, they usually become ingrained by the time adulthood is reached.

A Summary of Findings:

This chapter focused exclusively on non-Christian religions. If nothing else, our study verifies that all religions (except Christianity) reject the doctrine of the Trinity. In summary, the following represents a composite look at our findings of how the religions in this chapter regarded the Trinity.

God - Our findings indicate that many of the religions do acknowledge a God or gods in some form. Others maintain that the only thing necessary is a certain philosophy or lifestyle.

Jesus - As far as Jesus was concerned—some professed Him to be a messenger sent from God, a prophet, a good man, or an enlightened being, but not God in the flesh.

Holy Spirit - Perceived as an expression of God's love, an energy force, or some manifestation of a god from a previous state of existence.

Conflicting Findings Uncovered:

We now want to turn our attention to a different matter of concern. In examining the eight non-Christian religions, we came across some inconsistencies relating to the Trinity. Our findings disclosed that some of the religions regarded Jesus as a messenger of God, a prophet, a good man, or an enlightened being, but not God in the flesh. After careful consideration about these viewpoints, we find them to be confusing and conflicting. Therefore, we are including the following comments to address these concerns:

1. - *A Messenger, But Not God in the Flesh:*

First, let us consider the difficulty presented by calling Jesus a messenger sent from God, or a prophet. If Jesus was a messenger, or a prophet of God, His duty was to deliver the message God wanted us to hear. In other words, His message had to be true if it was from God. Therefore, if the message is true, we must believe all that He reported to us.

One of the things reported to us by Jesus is recorded in John 14:6. Jesus said, "I am the Way, the Truth, and the Life: no man cometh unto the Father, but by Me." If God gave Jesus this statement as a message for us, how then could we follow another way or religion? Obviously, it would be contradictory to say that Jesus was a messenger of God, or a prophet, and not believe His report. To do so would be calling God a liar.

2. - *A Good Man, But Not God in the Flesh*:

The second problem we found concerns those who hold to the opinion that Jesus was a good man, good teacher, or an enlightened being, but not God in the flesh. This belief sounds good until we realize what we are really saying, and that is, Jesus was the biggest liar to ever live. Why? Because He deceived over 2 billion people, now living, into believing He *is* God in the flesh. Not only that, He also deceived the multitudes who believed on Him since His time on earth.

Refusing to accept His deity, as well as His humanity, and then call Jesus a good man would be illogical indeed. Certainly a belief of this nature must be re-evaluated. Another item to consider—if Jesus was not part of the Godhead, the complete New Testament would be invalid since its contents are directed toward Him.

Issues Based on Faith:

Believing something without thought or consideration is undeniably foolish; yet, we have observed by analyzing the eight religions that this is exactly what many have done. The importance of the matter comes down to this: Either Jesus is God in the flesh and a part of the Godhead or He is not. By saying He is not, we must conclude that He could not have been a messenger from God or a good man. On the other hand, if we say He is, we are saying we believe He is the only begotten Son of God, and what He said to us is true.

As with God, everything regarding the issue of the Trinity is by faith and believing. Similarly, everything concerning Jesus is by faith and believing—the two cannot be separated. Much of the stigma associated with the Trinity happens from word of mouth or false teaching caused by misunderstanding.

Decision-Making with Careful Consideration:

Recall the verse of Scripture from the first paragraph of this chapter, "There is a way which seemeth right unto a man, but the end thereof *are* the ways of death." It becomes astounding when we consider all the various religions, philosophies, ideas, values, and beliefs we can explore. We can take note that any one of them may seem like the right way to go, but maybe not. Every person who passes through life on earth will have to make a decision. The questions they should ask are these: "Am I walking down the right path?" "How can I be sure?"

Summary of Chapter Five:

Many paths are available to us in our search for spiritual gratification. The question becomes, which path is the right one? Many times the path we take is the same one our parents took or one which tradition says is right. Religion is available in many forms. It can be a philosophy based on writings preserved in history. It can be the worship of anything connected to the force of nature. In some cases, it can even be anything that you would like it to be. The question remains, is it the right path?

The next chapter will provide us with a closer look at Christianity, considering it as the only religion to include the Trinity within its teachings.

Chapter 6

A Look at Christianity

Religion or Relationship:

Before we examine Christianity it may help to clarify one thing. As one would expect, when a person converts to Christianity he must leave his former religion. However, one exception is that of the Jew. The God of the Jew is the same God of the Christian. If a Jew came to accept Christ as his or her Messiah, that Jew would become a messianic Jew, a completed Jew or a Christian, whichever term the individual prefers.

Unlike other religions, an individual simply cannot join Christianity. Yes it's true; anyone can belong to a Christian Church, but that alone will not qualify him as a Christian. It is the Church's responsibility to explain how to become a Christian. Accordingly, the Word of God reveals that there is only one way an individual can become a Christian and that is by way of the new birth. We shall learn more about this occurrence later in this chapter as well as the next two chapters.

Christianity, although classified as a religion, does not refer to itself as a religion. Religion is a way devised by man to reach God and to achieve perfection through his own ability. In contrast, Christianity is a relationship with a Man named Jesus, called the Christ. Because of this relationship, the followers of Christ do not rely on man-made ideas, but upon the will of God as presented through the Scripture.

Because a person is a follower of Christ, he has come to be known as a Christian. The book of Acts records the following: "...it came to pass, that a whole year they assembled themselves with the Church, and taught much people. And the disciples were called Christians first in Antioch" Acts 11:26. The distinction of Christianity is that these individuals have made Jesus Christ the Lord of their lives. Thus, they have invoked a collective bond with like-minded believers in what they accept as truth and in Whom they worship.

The Three Sections of Christianity:

Founded upon the life and teachings of Jesus Christ around the year 30 A.D., Christianity now has numbers totaling nearly 2 billion people. Listed as one of the three major monotheistic world religions, the total Christian membership is divided into three major sectors: the Roman Catholic Church, Eastern Orthodox Church and Protestant churches. Catholicism accounts for about one half of the total Christian members.

The Birth of Christianity:

Jesus was born of a virgin, named Mary, around 4 A.D. in the town of Bethlehem in Judea. Mary was the espoused wife of a man named Joseph and both were of the house of David. The angel Gabriel appeared to Mary and told her she would conceive a Son by the Holy Ghost. He would be called Jesus, meaning Savior, and heir to the throne of His father David.

Jesus was 30 years of age when He began His ministry. Many of His teachings centered on *the Kingdom of God*. Yet, what He taught upset many of the Jewish religious, especially His claim that He was the only way to God the Father and salvation. They were looking for a Messiah, but the values taught by Jesus were contrary to many of their laws. Obviously troubled by it, they plotted to kill Him. As it turned out, an apostle of Christ named Judas, agreed to betray Jesus for thirty pieces of silver.

Condemned to Die:

The betrayal of Jesus lead to His arrest and a sentence of death. He was tortured and beaten, spat upon, mocked, made to carry a cross, stripped of His clothes and hanged on the cross until He died. Then, just to make sure He was dead, they pierced His side with a spear at which point blood and water issued forth. Many miracles and healings were attributed to Him in the three years before His crucifixion and death. He predicted that He would die and rise again, and, as it happened, He rose from the dead after three days, just as He prophesied.

After His Resurrection:

Jesus appeared to His disciples several times following the resurrection. On one occasion, He assigned to them *the Great Commission* to go and teach all nations, baptizing them in the name of the Father, and of the Son, and of the Holy Ghost, teaching them to observe all the things that He taught them to do. Then the disciples watched as Jesus ascended into heaven. Ten days later, the disciples received power by the Holy Ghost while in an upper room in Jerusalem. Imbued with power, they went forth preaching the good news of the Gospel throughout the land. This new teaching spread rapidly, yet much persecution soon followed.

Dedicated Men Persisted:

Christianity finally took hold throughout the Roman Empire because dedicated men of passion persisted in proclaiming the Gospel message. After the death of the Apostles, the writings they left behind helped confirm the information needed to design the doctrines and specifications for the Church. Of the final twelve Apostles (including Paul), only John did not die a martyr's death, but he was exiled to the Isle of Patmos where he died of old age. The fact that all twelve men were willing to lay down their lives, rather than deny Jesus and His teachings, reinforced the legitimacy of Christ's deity.

Doctrinal Differences Arise:

Over time, differences of opinion began to appear. Disagreements relating to the teaching of the Trinity were the major cause of discord, and many would not accept its doctrine. Councils met to study the differences and to establish standards for the Church. These standards reinforced and justified the teaching of the Trinity. Although differences and divisions have transpired over the years, most arose over the issue of whether faith or works merited salvation. The dogma of the Trinity is still intact today with little change from its original description.

Guidelines and Ceremonies:

In the last chapter, we found that most religions base the foundation of their existence on certain rules and guidelines of their founder. The foundation for Christianity is Jesus Christ Himself. The Holy Bible contains the rules and guidelines, which Christians believe to be the authenticated Word of God. The body of Christian believers is called the Church, and the place of worship is in a building called a *church*.

Worship comes in many forms—prayer, singing, chanting, and music. Rituals include: Communion, marriage, baptism in water, communal worship and burial. Prayer, Bible studies and worship services constitute ceremonies for Christians. The blessed hope of the Church is that someday Christ will return for them, and they will live and reign with Him forever.

Christianity's "Born-Again" Experience:

As mentioned earlier, an individual cannot become a Christian merely by joining a Christian Church. He must be born into Christianity. Like the Trinity, the term "born-again" is another unique aspect of the Christian life. For a person to become a genuine Christian, he must first undergo a life-changing occurrence called *the new birth experience*.

Jesus was conveying this information to a man named Nicodemus, a ruler of the Jews. Jesus said to Nicodemus, "...Verily, verily, I say unto thee, Except a man be born again, he cannot see the kingdom of God" John 3:3. Nicodemus was unable to understand what Jesus meant by the term "born-again." However, Jesus told Nicodemus that "born-again" did not constitute the physical act of rebirth as from the womb, but a totally new rebirth of the spirit. Recall in an earlier chapter regarding spiritual death—in essence, "born-again" is the only means by which we can become spiritually alive.

The Encounter:

For an individual to meet with this *new birth experience,* two things must take place:

1. The individual must repent (*have a changed heart and desire to be changed*). The Bible states, "Let the wicked forsake his way..." Isaiah 55:7. Another Scripture passage reveals, "For all have all sinned, and come short of the glory of God" Romans 3:23. Repentance, therefore, is the forsaking of our sinful ways.
2. The individual must call upon the name of Jesus Christ, and invite Him to become Lord and Savior.

When we make these two decisions on our part, God takes over on His part. Our part is to initiate the decision and desire for salvation. God will not violate our free will, but He awaits an invitation from us. When we have repented and invited Jesus to be our Lord, we are "born-again" according to the Scriptures.

The Bible says, "That if thou shalt confess with thy mouth the Lord Jesus, and shalt believe in thine heart that God hath raised Him from the dead, thou shalt be saved" Romans 10:9. By affirming that we are sinners in need of forgiveness, and calling upon the name of the Lord, we indicate our need for salvation.

The Scriptures reveal that there is only one place to find salvation. In reference to Jesus, Acts 4:12 states, "Neither is there salvation in any other: for there is none other name under heaven given among men, whereby we must be saved."

The Simplicity:

It is noteworthy to mention the simplicity of the "born-again" experience. God takes us right where we are with what is in our heart. No works are involved and no requirement to be a good person or to belong to a certain religion. The Bible says, "For whosoever shall call upon the name of the Lord shall be saved" Romans 10:13. Thus, the simplicity of *the new birth*.

The New Life:

When we make the choice to repent and to call upon the name of the Lord, the Spirit of God takes up residence in our heart. A life-changing event takes place when the Holy Spirit comes into a person's life. Love replaces hate, faith replaces fear, and hope replaces despair. Consequently, the individual receives the renewed life that replaces death. The guidance of the Spirit and the desire to serve God take precedence over sin, and hence, the term "born-again" finds its meaning.

The Challenge:

Is this "born-again" phenomenon for real? Well, there is one sure way to find out and that is by trying it. Only Christianity recognizes the reality of *the new birth* and it alone can make this challenge.

Why does Christianity offer such a challenge? For one thing, the challenge is to prove that Jesus Christ is the one true way back to God. For sure, other religions make this claim, but no other religion offers to back up their claim. Christianity offers to back up its claim with proof. How then does the "born-again" experience verify its authenticity, and what is the proof?

You Can Know For Sure:
The answer is—the transformed life. The "change" experienced by the person provides the evidence of *the new birth*. When the Spirit of God takes up residence within the heart, there is no mistaking the "born-again" encounter. The evidence of *the new birth* exists within the individual, while the change is evident to those around him. In actual fact, the proof is in the heart.

Divisions of Christianity:
Roman Catholic Church: The largest of the three major Church groups within Christianity, the Roman Catholic Church, consists of Christians who accept the absolute authority of the bishop of Rome (the pope), regarding Church matters.

The word "catholic," meaning universal, was the designated name adopted by the early Church when it began. The largest numbers of Catholics are in Europe and Latin America, but large memberships also exist in other parts of the world. Vatican City is the papal state within Rome and serves as the center of operations for the Church government and the pope.

Besides the pope, higher dignitaries include clergy called cardinals, which are selected by the pope. In turn, at the death or resignation of a pope, the conclave of cardinals meet in Vatican City to elect the new pope.

Other clergy include archbishops, bishops, and priests. Priests generally shepherd a parish, while bishops oversee a diocese consisting of a group of parishes.

Members of the religious orders are nuns, brothers and laity. They staff schools, hospitals and other social services. Outreaches include missionary work to the poor, the homeless, in prisons and hospitals and in remote areas of the world.

Worship in Catholicism is generally by way of the Mass, which is a commemorative celebration of the sacrificial offering of the body and blood of Christ. Rituals include the seven sacraments that Catholics experience at various stages of their lives. All ordained clergy administer the sacraments and rites of the Church. There are several special days called "holy days" observed throughout the year in celebration of certain Church events exclusive to Catholicism.

Although differences do exist, for the most part, the Roman Church's doctrine is in step with other Christian ideology. The Roman Catholic Church establishes its doctrines on the Bible and Church traditions. Included within these doctrines is the complete recognition of the Trinity.

The following constitutes some of the disagreement that exist relating to the teachings and beliefs of Catholicism and the other branches of Christianity. They include: the authority of the pope, salvation by works, dissimilarities in the Communion offering, celebration of the Mass, confession of sins, prayers to saints and the doctrine of purgatory.

Orthodox Church: Found mainly in Greece, Russia, Eastern Europe and Western Asia, the Orthodox churches are united by common beliefs and formalities. Total membership is over 130 million persons. The Church ratified its doctrines and beliefs through the Bible and traditions. Early Church writings and council decrees established the Church's authority and by-laws.

The split between the Eastern and Western churches occurred in 1054 A.D., although a rift began hundreds of years earlier. Generally considered as the major causes of the break are two religious issues. One issue was the phrase included in the Nicene-Constantinopolitan creed, asserting that the Holy Spirit proceeds from the Father. The other issue disputed the authority of the Roman pope over the Eastern Church. The Orthodox Church considers no one person in the Church as infallible.

Church services center on hymns, prayers and the Bible. Services include, the *Divine Liturgy*, which is a celebration of the Eucharist, the *Divine Office*, and *Occasional Offices*, which includes services for baptism and marriage. Church buildings are richly decorated with religious art. Rituals of the seven sacraments are similar to ones used by Roman Catholicism and form an important element in Church customs.

Protestant Church: Protestantism developed out of the Reformation period, initiated by Martin Luther, in the 16th century. Luther, a monk who meant to reform the Church, challenged the Roman Church authorities on matters regarding salvation. He interpreted certain New Testament passages to mean that God's grace alone was the source of salvation, while Rome proclaimed salvation by good works. The dispute led to Luther's excommunication from the Roman Church.

Eventually, new denominations emerged and were classed under the division of Christianity known as Protestantism. Today there are many such Christian denominations under the umbrella of Protestantism. These organizations are not under the authority of the Roman pope, but each denomination is independently governed by a board of administrators who oversee the business of their collective Church body.

In the individual churches, a leader, called the pastor, is in charge of Church affairs. Rituals include: Communion, baptism, marriage and burial procedures. In Protestantism, the issue of the Trinity generally agrees with the tenets of the Roman Catholic Church. Many churches have outreach programs, which include missionary work overseas, to prisons, to the poor or homeless, and to hospitals.

Some of the larger organizations formed from the Reformation were the Baptist, Episcopal, Lutheran, Methodist, Presbyterian, and Pentecostal churches. However, there are many other denominations worldwide, both large and small, included under the designation of Protestantism. Above and beyond these organizations are several non-Trinitarian denominations. These churches generally rely on other documents interpreted by their founder, which overshadow the contents of the Bible.

The Great Commission:
Jesus gave His disciples the commandment to go out and teach all nations and be a witness for Him. This is understood to be the role of Christianity. As those disciples evangelized the nations in their day, so it is that the same obligation is extended to Christianity today. Nevertheless, as persecution abounded in the New Testament age, so also persecution abounds in our generation. The fact is, more Christians have been martyred in our era than in any other period in Church history.

Summary of Chapter Six:
Christianity was founded by Jesus Christ around the year 30 A.D. when He began teaching that the Kingdom of God was at hand. Because of His teachings, He was despised by the religious leaders and they plotted to kill Him. The betrayal by one of His disciples led to His crucifixion on a cross. He predicted His resurrection from the dead, which occurred three days later. Before His ascension into heaven Jesus gave His disciples *the Great Commission*, which they loyally honored.

Jesus, the second Person of the Trinity, is the focal point of all celebrations, religious observances, rituals and worship services. The spirit of unity attained by the New Testament Church is a priority and the desire of the Church of today.

Chapter 7

The Trinity's Central Objective

Violated Law:
We cannot fully realize the Trinity and the need for a Savior without coming to terms with Satan's true objective in the "Garden of Eden." His obvious motive was to bring about sin, but as we shall find out, this was not his only intent. The first chapter of Genesis discloses the granting of dominion authority to man. In doing so, God made man responsible for all earthly matters. The only condition placed on Adam was to abstain from the forbidden fruit. At the same time, embedded within this condition, was man's right to choose. Thus, by acquiring the freedom to choose, he was free to partake of the forbidden fruit or to abstain from it.

When God created the universe, He set certain ethical and comprehensive guidelines in place. Since God made man in His own image and likeness and placed him in such high authority on the earth, the rules relating to man are firm. One thing is certain, these regulations are for our protection. Nevertheless, sin invaded the heart of Adam, the first man, and in so doing, set off a series of events. God absolutely had the power and capacity to intervene when Adam and Eve disobeyed, but by doing so, He would have intruded on the very directive He had set in place. That principle declares, "The soul that sinneth, it shall die" Ezekiel 18:4, and "The wages of sin is death..." Romans 6:23.

Man in Bondage:

As a fallen angel, Satan was fully aware of the consequences of disobeying God. He had held a high position among the ranks of the angels. Therefore, being in such high standing, not only was he aware of God's laws, but he also was conscious of God's integrity. He knew that God holds firm to His Word. By deceiving Adam and Eve, not only did Satan tempt them to sin, but he also achieved his true purpose, which was to seize the earthly dominion. This came about when Adam disregarded God's directive. Adam no longer remained obedient to God. Now he assumed obedience to Satan.

What resulted from this act continues to haunt man, even to this day. As it happened, another precept was violated, which placed man under the control of Satan. The following Scripture verses may shed some light on this principle:

- Jesus answered them, Verily, verily, I say unto you, Whosoever committeth sin is the servant of sin. - (John 8:34)

- ...to whom ye yield yourselves servants to obey, his servants ye are to whom ye obey; whether of sin unto death, or of obedience unto righteousness? - (Romans 6:16)

- He that committeth sin is of the devil; - (1 John 3:8)

No Way Out for Humanity?

Thus, we discover that man was disobedient to God by submitting to Satan's deception. In turn, this produced the transfer of dominion authority from man to Satan. In the exchange, man became servant to Satan. The situation created by sin took on an appearance of hopelessness. Not only did sin bring forth death, but man essentially became slave to Satan. Was there any possible way for redemption back to God? After careful analysis, there was a way, but only *one* way. Still, that way seemed impossible in the eyes of man. Only a human being, free from bondage to Satan and sin, would be able to redeem mankind.

Humanity Doomed?

Since Adam had no children before the fall, there were no other sinless people on earth. Furthermore, Adam's descendants would all acquire his sinful nature. Without a person who was free of sin available to deliver man from his despair, humanity was doomed. Satan gained control of the dominion authority over the earth, and *fallen man* was placed under the authority of the *fallen angel*.

The Father of Lies:

- Ye are of *your* father the devil, and the lusts of your father ye will do. He was a murderer from the beginning, and abode not in the truth, because there is no truth in him. When he speaketh a lie, he speaketh of his own: for he is a liar, and the father of it. - (John 8:44)

The above Scripture illustrates that man transferred his loyalty from God to Satan. Jesus was speaking to the religious leaders when He made this statement. If the religious superiors were children of the devil, where did everyone else stand? If Satan is our father, then God cannot be our Father.

Satan's Authority Undisputed:

We find another piece of evidence to back up the claim of Satan's authority. At one point, Satan tempted Jesus while He was in the wilderness. In the following Scripture passages, we find Satan offering Jesus all the kingdoms of the world if He would only bow down to him. Although He did not give in to the temptations of Satan, Jesus also did not dispute Satan's claim to the dominion authority.

- And the devil, taking Him up into an high mountain, showed unto Him all the kingdoms of the world in a moment of time. - (Luke 4:5)
- And the devil said unto Him, All this power will I give Thee, and the glory of them: for that is delivered unto me; and to whomsoever I will I give it. - (Luke 4:6)
- If Thou therefore wilt worship me, all shall be Thine. - (Luke 4:7)

The Result of Obedience to Satan:

If Jesus had agreed to Satan's request, He would have fallen into the same trap as Adam. By submitting to Satan's temptations, Jesus would have been disobedient to His Father's will. Notwithstanding, Satan would be under no obligation to fulfill his end of the bargain, since he is the Father of Lies and void of any moral standards to live by.

God's Answer for Man:

In examining the situation, only a human being, not connected to the lineage of Adam, would qualify to restore man back to God. This is not all—the individual must be without sin to gain back the dominion authority from Satan. The big question was—where would he come from? Angels or beasts could not become eligible because they were not human beings, nor made in the image and likeness of God. That meant there was no one left to redeem fallen man from his bondage.

God may have been in heaven, but He was fully aware of the desperate situation of man. He also knew that man had no way out of his difficulty. Still, despite man's unfaithfulness, God's love for humanity did not stop. For man, that was good news, because God had an answer to the problem. The question was: What was that answer and just how did God propose to accomplish His plan?

What Was God's Answer?

After analyzing every possible option available, it turns out that there were no available options, but one. That one ultimate answer was—God Himself. God devised a plan whereby He would come down to this earth to redeem fallen man from his plight and make a way for restoration. In light of the fact that no other perfect beings existed anywhere in the whole universe, God truly was the only answer to man's predicament.

Hope for humanity was now in the hands of a merciful God. Yet, how would He achieve this feat? The Bible tells us that no man can look upon God and live, Exodus 33:20. If that was the case, God could never come down to earth to live among mortal man. Nevertheless, with God all things are possible.

- I will ransom them from the power of the grave; I will redeem them from death; O death: I will be thy plagues; O grave, I will be thy destruction: repentance shall be hid from Mine eyes. - (Hosea 13:14)

Prophecies Regarding the Messiah:

Throughout the history of the Old Testament, God revealed certain prophecies to various individuals. The first one was presented to Satan in the "Garden," where He prophesied that the seed of the woman would bruise Satan's head. God also promised a Messiah would come from the seed of Abraham, Isaac and Jacob, and He would be from the tribe of Judah.

The Kingdom of this coming Messiah would be established forever upon the throne of David, and He would be born in the town of Bethlehem. Moreover, He would be born of a virgin and called the mighty God and Immanuel (God with us).

These prophecies were there, open for all to see, and certainly Satan was aware of each and every one.

- Of the increase of *His* government and peace *there shall be* no end, upon the throne of David.... - (Isaiah 9:7)

- Therefore the Lord Himself shall give you a sign; Behold a virgin shall conceive, and bear a Son, and shall call His name Immanuel. - (Isaiah 7:14)

Jesus—His Lineage Through God:

When the time came, God chose a virgin, named Mary, whose family tree went through King David back to Jacob, Isaac and Abraham. Even Joseph, Mary's espoused husband, traced his lineage back to David and Abraham. An angel named Gabriel appeared to Mary and told her that the Holy Ghost would come upon her and overshadow her, and she would conceive and be with Child. The Child she would bear would be from God. She was to call His name Jesus, and He would be born in the town of Bethlehem. Similarly, the angel also appeared to Joseph.

- But thou, Bethlehem Ephratah, *though* thou be little among the thousands of Judea, *yet* out of thee shall He come forth unto Me *that is* to be ruler in Israel; whose goings forth *have been* from of old, from everlasting. - (Micah 5:2)

Jesus Met the Requirements:

What took place at the birth of Jesus is quite significant, in contrast to what took place in the "Garden of Eden." God's strategy to redeem fallen humanity involved using a virgin, of the lineage of David, of the tribe of Judah, as the instrument to bring forth His only begotten Son into the world. By using a woman, God fulfilled the requirement of belonging to the human race. The fact that her ancestry went back to Abraham, Isaac and Jacob satisfied the covenant God made with them. Because she was carrying a Child conceived by the Holy Ghost insured that Jesus was of God, and He was the perfect Being needed to restore fallen man.

- For unto us a Child is born, unto us a Son is given: and the government shall be upon His shoulder: and His name shall be called Wonderful, Counselor, The mighty God, The everlasting Father, The Prince of Peace. - (Isaiah 9:6)

The Only Begotten Son:

As it was, the Child met every requirement necessary to become a human being. Whereas the ancestry goes back through the father, Jesus was not linked to the bloodline of man through Adam, rather He was the offspring of God.

Because Adam was a created being, all of the children of Adam would become created beings as well. This is significant because Jesus was not created—His Father was not of the lineage of Adam, making Jesus the first-born of God. Thus, Jesus has the distinction of being called the only begotten Son of God. In addition, since the Holy Ghost was His Father, His blood was not stained by sin.

- I will declare the decree: the Lord hath said unto Me. Thou art My Son; this day have I begotten Thee. - (Psalms 2:7)

A View of the Cross:

Jesus fulfilled all the conditions needed to redeem fallen humanity; yet, He had a lifetime to complete His mission without dishonoring His Father. He was fully Man and therefore subject to the same temptations and hindrances as everyone else.

- Seeing then that we have a great high priest, that is passed into the heavens, Jesus the Son of God, let us hold fast *our* profession. - (Hebrews 4:14)
- For we have not an high priest which cannot be touched with the feeling of our infirmities; but was in all points tempted like as *we are, yet* without sin. - (Hebrews 4:15)

Even so, in leaving His "glorious estate" and His "majestic throne," He fashioned Himself and became obedient even to death on the cross.

The Book of Isaiah gives a better portrayal of what Jesus went through to redeem fallen humanity.

- Behold, My servant shall deal prudently, He shall be exalted and extolled, and be very high. - (Isaiah 52:13)
- As many were astonied at Thee; His visage was so marred more than any man, and His form more than the sons of men. - (Isaiah 52:14)

- He is despised and rejected of men; a man of sorrows, and acquainted with grief: and we hid as it were *our* faces from Him; He was despised, and we esteemed Him not. - (Isaiah 53:3)
- Surely He hath borne our griefs, and carried our sorrows: yet we did esteem Him stricken, smitten of God, and afflicted. - (Isaiah 53:4)
- But He *was* wounded for our transgressions, *He was* bruised for our iniquities: the chastisement of our peace *was* upon Him; and with His stripes we are healed. - (Isaiah 53:5)
- All we like sheep have gone astray; we have turned every one to his own way; and the LORD hath laid on Him the iniquity of us all. - (Isaiah 53:6)

This report from the book of Isaiah, chapters 52 and 53, generates a dramatic picture of what Jesus went through as He endured the cross. Moreover, Isaiah 53:10 says, "it yet pleased the LORD to bruise Him; He hath put *Him* to grief: when Thou shalt make His soul an offering for sin...." God's only begotten Son was made an offering for sin, yet it pleased God because it gave fallen humanity a means to return to Him.

God Became the WAY:

Although the one bruised was Jesus (God's only begotten Son), He is no less a part of the same Godhead as the Father. As we progress further into our study, and as we uncover more of the Trinity, this matter will become more obvious. What we want to realize now is the purpose and the manner used by God to compensate for the wrong done by man.

Finding a WAY to redeem man, where there seemed to be no way, gives greater credibility to the fact that with God all things are possible. The reality that it pleased God to become that WAY gives even greater proof of His love for man.

- Greater love hath no man than this, that a man lay down his life for his friends. - (John 15:13)

His Humanity, Not His Divinity:

The purpose of the incarnation of Jesus was not to show Himself as God, but as He said, to redeem the lost sheep of the house of Israel. However, as destiny would have it, the Israelites rejected Christ, which resulted in salvation being extended also to the Gentiles. Accordingly, now everyone is eligible to receive God's deliverance from sin.

While it was within His ability to perform great miracles, such as calling down fire from the sky to convince the people He was God, that certainly was not His intent. His objective involved His humanity, not His divinity. Jesus told His disciples that He could ask of the Father and He would send down twelve legions of angels to save Him from the cross. However, the cross was the very reason He had come to earth.

- For the preaching of the cross is to them that perish foolishness, but unto us which are saved it is the power of God. - (1 Corinthians 1:18)

In the Final Hours:

To say that the final hours in the life of the Redeemer were unimaginable is an understatement. The punishment that He endured is beyond words to describe. Satan, *the prince of this world*, was jubilant in thinking he had contained this God-Man in what seemed to be Jesus's final demise. By entering into Judas (an apostle of Jesus), Satan set up a series of events, which led to the sentence of death for his Arch-rival (Jesus). This was an attempt to force Jesus into a rebellious situation— one that would be contrary to the will of His Father.

Satan was unsuccessful when he tempted Jesus in the wilderness, but this time he was determined not to fail. Satan had no claim on Jesus since Jesus was not of the ancestry of Adam, but if Satan could get Jesus to be disloyal to the Father, his evil scheme would succeed.

Thirty Pieces of Silver:

Judas agreed to betray Jesus for thirty pieces of silver, thereby opening himself up to satanic control. That betrayal led to the arrest of Jesus and culminated in His eventual crucifixion upon the cross. Soon Satan (the demonic inventor of evil) would presume triumph is certain. Defeating Jesus would be the ultimate victory, and he would reign supreme. God's own law gives the assurance. Still, Satan, so accustomed to deceiving his prey and winning, forgot to allow for one small detail. What if Jesus did not rebel against the will of His Father? In all likelihood that factor did not even enter into the picture.

Defeat Appears Certain:

Jesus endured all the pain and suffering man could provide. In spite of that, He carried all of our sorrows, all of our grief, and all of our iniquities within His own body. While Jesus was on the cross and close to death, Satan was lurking in the background waiting his chance to mock and ridicule.

- And being found in fashion as a Man, He humbled Himself, and became obedient unto death, even the death of the cross. - (Philippians 2:8)

Sinless Man Forsaken:
Then came the cry from the cross, "Eloi, Eloi, lama sabachthani?" which is, being interpreted, "My God, My God, why hast Thou forsaken Me?" When He had spoken this, He bore the sins of the world upon Himself. This event marked the first time Jesus called His Father God. Recall the Scripture, "Thou art of purer eyes than to behold evil, and canst not look on inequity..." Habakkuk 1:13. With the weight of sin upon Him, God could no longer behold His Son. From all appearances, it looked as if His Father had deserted Him.

- My God, My God, why hast Thou forsaken Me? *why art Thou* so far from helping Me, *and from* the words of My roaring? - (Psalms 22:1)

The Penalty Paid:
Sin came with a penalty, and that penalty was death. At death, the soul of man takes his sins to the regions of hell where the punishment is apportioned.

When Jesus cried out for the last time and said, "It is finished"; "Father, into Thy hands I commend My Spirit," the mission on earth was completed. Yet another mission was in the making. Jesus took the sins of the world upon Himself, but that alone did not pay the penalty. Those sins could not simply remain on Jesus—the full penalty needed reparation.

- Thou hast laid Me in the lowest pit, in darkness, in the deeps. Thou hast put away Mine aquaintance far from Me; ... Lord I have called daily upon Thee, I have stretched out My hands unto Thee. - (Psalms 88:6&8,9)

Dominion Over the Whole Earth:

While Jesus was on the cross, He remarked to a thief who was on a cross next to Him, "...Today shalt thou be with Me in paradise." Acts 2:25-31 and Ephesians 4:9-10 also note that Jesus descended into the lower reaches of the earth, the location of hell. Yet another Scripture, Revelation 1:18, announces that Jesus has the keys to hell and of death.

We can only assume from these Scriptures that Jesus descended into the lower parts of the earth, to the place called hell, or the place of the dead. There He deposited the sins of mankind. Satan met Him there with victory in his eyes. However, since Jesus was an innocent man and now in control of dominion authority, Satan's victory plans were about to change.

Dominion authority applied not only to the surface of the earth, but also to the whole earth. Since the location of hell is in the earth, it is included, as verified by the fact that Jesus now has the keys. While in hell, Jesus not only recovered the keys of hell and death, but He also set the captives free.

- For Thou wilt not leave My soul in hell; neither wilt Thou suffer Thine Holy One to see corruption. - (Psalms 16:10) and (Acts 2:27)

- And the graves were opened; and many bodies of the saints which slept arose, - (Matthew 27:52)
- And came out of the graves after His resurrection, and went into the holy city, and appeared to many. - (Matthew 27:53)

Legal Authority Undisputed:

It was all over, and Satan became the loser. By killing an innocent man, Satan himself violated a law of divine justice. For this reason, Jesus invalidated Satan's legal claim to the authority and established salvation for humanity.

By virtue of obedience unto death, the outcome of the victorious conquest is undisputed. Jesus achieved complete repossession of the dominion authority.

Jesus in the Form of God:

- Who, being in the form of God, thought it not robbery to be equal with God: - (Philippians 2:6)
- But made Himself of no reputation, and took upon Him the form of a servant, and was made in the likeness of men: - (Philippians 2:7)
- And being found in fashion as a man, He humbled Himself, and became obedient unto death, even the death of the cross. - (Philippians 2:8)
- Wherefore God also hath highly exalted Him, and given Him a name which is above every name: - (Philippians 2:9)
- That at the name of Jesus every knee should bow, of *things* in heaven, and things in earth, and *things* under the earth; - (Philippians 2:10)
- And *that* every tongue should confess that Jesus Christ is Lord, to the glory of God the Father. - (Philippians 2:11)

Who Killed Christ:

We must take note that no one person, or group, caused the death of Christ on the cross, but it was by the hand of Satan. All who sin are responsible in partaking of His death. Therefore, the entire human race is equally guilty. Jesus willingly paid the penalty, or He would not have elected to do so.

The King of kings and Lord of lords:

In His first coming, He became our Redeemer and our Savior. When He comes again, He will be King of kings and Lord of lords.

- O give thanks to the **Lord of lords**: for His mercy *endureth* for ever. - (Psalms 136:3)

- ...until the appearing of our Lord Jesus Christ: Which in His times He shall show *Who is* the blessed and the only Potentate, the **King of kings, and Lord of lords**; - (1 Timothy 6:14,5)

- ...and the Lamb shall overcome them: for He is **Lord of lords and King of kings**.... - (Revelation 17:14)

Exposing Satan:

The evil one has been defeated, but his attacks did not stop. He knows that Jesus is the only way to salvation and does everything in his power to hinder the proclamation of the gospel. How does he do this? By using sinful man, who even now is under his control. Unlike God, Satan cannot be everywhere at once, but he is the fallen angel who deceived one third of the heavenly host. These fallen angels are also under his dominance and do his bidding throughout the earth. Working constantly, they go about deceiving those who are willing and vulnerable. 1 Peter 5:8 describes the adversary the devil, as a roaring lion, walking about, seeking whom he may devour.

The Bible says that even the devils believe and they tremble. They understand their fate and the closeness of the hour. Although he is unable to defeat Jesus, Satan has a clear objective, and that is to take as many with him as possible.

The Bible again asserts that Satan sometimes masquerades as an angel of light. Jesus declared that Satan only comes to steal, kill and destroy. He stole the dominion authority from man, he was responsible for the killing of Jesus, and he wants to take mankind to the same destination that's in store for him.

- For we wrestle not against flesh and blood, but against principalities, against powers, against the rulers of the darkness of this world, against spiritual wickedness in high *places.* - (Ephesians 6:12)

Jesus defeated Satan in his own game plan. Truth overcame lies, good overcame evil, life overcame death, mercy overcame wickedness, and love overcame hate. That's not all—Jesus said the gates of hell shall not prevail against His Church.

Summary of Chapter Seven:

God granted the dominion authority to man, with one stipulation, he was not to eat of the forbidden fruit. Satan, in deceiving man, not only caused him to sin, but also achieved his real motive, which was to take control of the dominion authority. In reality, man became Satan's slave by obeying Satan's deception. Man was in need of a way back to God, but only a sinless individual could meet the requirements.

One thing is evident in this chapter and that is the love God has for man. God knew of man's plight and devised a way for man to be redeemed. God's answer was—God Himself. The result— He suffered all the grief and agony man could bestow on Him, yet He overcame it all and became the sacrifice for man's redemption. Still, although Jesus recovered the dominion authority, it did not erase man's freedom to choose.

Chapter 8

The Trinity and Salvation

The Trinity—Central to Salvation:
From the information we received in the preceding chapter, the purpose of the Trinity is obvious. Every aspect acknowledges the Trinity's creditability in securing our salvation. As John 3:16 so powerfully discloses, "For God so loved the world, that He gave His only begotten Son, that whosoever believeth in Him should not perish, but have everlasting life." Still, for a savior to fulfill his purpose, there must be someone in need of salvation with a desire to be saved.

Clearly, we have determined that everyone in the human race is in need of a Savior. Since the Trinity was earmarked for saving mankind, we have set aside this chapter to pinpoint some of the details surrounding God's redemption of man. Several points are provided to help identify the importance and the simplicity of salvation.

Man's Right to Choose:
Before we venture too far, we must clarify one thing. The fact of the cross and Christ's victory over Satan creates the appearance of automatic freedom from the consequences of sin. However, this simply is not so. Because man has a free will, he is free to choose whom he wants to serve, and it is up to each individual to make that choice.

Through sin, man acquired a sinful nature. In contrast, Jesus lived a sinless life on earth and did not acquire a sin-nature. Considering the sin-nature of man, what Jesus did at Calvary did not change the basic structure of man. Indeed, Christ took the sins of the whole world and paid the penalty for them. Nonetheless, nothing has changed until the individual makes the decision to transfer his obedience from Satan back to God.

Man's Framework and God's Spirit:
The composition of man did not change after the cross. If we look again at the structure of man's existence, we discover the following principles at work. The body still houses the soul and spirit, the blood continues to be the life of the flesh, and the bloodline extends back to Adam. Moreover, man retained the knowledge of good and evil, with the ability to sin. The penalty of death is yet the consequence of sin, and freedom of choice, as well as separation from the Spirit of God, still exists.

The Justice of God:
As indicated earlier, the deity of God could not simply redeem fallen man. To do so would have violated God's own ethical standards. The question we must ask: If God utterly took back the dominion authority from Satan and gave it back to man, what happens when man sins again? When we recognize the justice of God, which dictates that even though the authority at that time belonged to Satan (the evil one), God will not violate His own laws. In view of that, God could not redeem man with His deity. The Savior had to belong to the human race in order to redeem humanity.

The Offering for Sin:
Divine justice also demands that the penalty for sin be paid. If Jesus had not taken our sins and deposited them in hell, He would still be in possession of them today. The following Scriptures disclose that Jesus no longer carries those sins.

- And ye know that He was manifested to take away our sins; and **in Him is no sin**. - (1 John 3:5)

- So Christ was once offered to bear the sins of many; and unto them that look for Him shall He appear the second time **without sin** unto salvation. - (Hebrews 9:28)

When an individual rejects the salvation of God through Christ, the penalty for his sins remains unpaid.

- Therefore they say unto God, Depart from us; for we desire not the knowledge of Thy ways. - (Job 21:14)

This means that, in due time, the individual must make payment for sins himself. Making the decision to pay for the sins himself, also expresses a desire to keep Satan as master. So, at the death of the individual, Satan becomes his or her master for eternity.

- He that committeth sin is of the devil; for the devil sinneth from the beginning. For this purpose the Son of God was manifested, that He might destroy the works of the devil. - (1 John 3:8)

The Individual's Choice:

At the same time we must ask; What good was the cross? Well, one striking detail is that Christ recovered the dominion authority from Satan. Now it is possible for man to regain access to it, but only if he so chooses. The individual has retained the knowledge of good and evil, and for that reason he continues to be subject to Satan's temptations. If, by preference of the individual, he wishes to stay with Satan, he has that right. Even so, by making a choice to stay with Satan, declares he is willing to accept what Satan has to offer, namely *death, hell* and the *grave*.

Aware of the Cross:

Before the cross, mankind was limited to one choice. However, Satan and death are no longer the only viable option. The achievement of Calvary opened the door to another selection. We can now choose to become sons of God by acknowledging the triumph of the cross, and Christ as the One who fulfilled it.

- But as many as received Him, to them gave He power to become the sons of God, *even* to them that believe on His name: - (John 1:12)

Reaching God Through Adam's Lineage:

If each person were to follow his or her ancestry back, eventually each would wind up at Adam. Adam would be the last stop before God. However, we cannot get to God through Adam because of inherited sin. No matter how good we are, and no matter how many good works we do, we will always fall short of God and His glory. As a result, we can never return to God through the lineage of Adam, or by our own efforts.

Remember that man is also a trinity. He exists in body, soul and spirit. His ancestry back to Adam is both physical and spiritual. In view of that, let's examine what the cross of Calvary enables fallen man to do.

The Cross is a Shortcut:

Essentially, we can think the cross as a bridge or a shortcut back to God. From our perspective with Adam, we are looking back in time, and our genealogy records a long list of ancestors in our attempt to reach God. With the cross we look forward in time, and we have a direct path to God. Looking back in time, we notice our father, our forefathers and of course, our father Satan. However, when we take the shortcut to God and we look forward, we find something very significant. Through the cross, we are connected directly to our true Father.

Changes Made Through the Cross:

Because of the cross we are no longer blocked by Adam's ancestry to reach God. Now we have direct access to God through Jesus. Our spirit receives life through the Spirit of God. Moreover, the blood of Jesus cleanses us from all unrighteousness. As we discovered in the Book of Acts 17:26, the blood of all mankind originated with Adam. With the cross, when we become "born-again," we inherit a new bloodline through the blood of Christ.

Heredity Simplified:

With bondage to Satan broken and the ancestry simplified, the shortcut to God extends from the individual, through the Holy Spirit, to Jesus, to God. This simplified method indicates the individual is a child of God and belongs to the family of God.

Bondage to Satan is Broken:

Disobedience caused separation from God; however, acceptance reunites us to God. Deliverance supplies assurance that bondage to Satan no longer exists and the yoke of oppression has departed. Certainly there are trials and temptations even as before. The difference is, Satan no longer has authority over us, but we gained authority over Satan. The following depicts the decree of the "born-again" individual: Jesus said, "...In the world ye shall have tribulation: but be of good cheer; I have overcome the world. - (John 16:33)

The Trinity at Work:

Let's examine the Trinity in man at the point of salvation. When the unsaved person repents and invites Jesus in as his Lord, we find the following situation taking place:

1. The individual calls upon the name of Jesus for salvation.
2. The Holy Spirit creates life in the spirit of the individual.
3. Light expels darkness and life extracts death.
4. The love of God fills the soul.

Herein is the lifeline of God the Holy Spirit, extended through God the Son, to God the Father. Thus, receiving salvation brings illumination to the Trinity.

How is Salvation Attained?

We now have an idea how this life-changing event occurs in conjunction with salvation. The question becomes—How do we bring about these changes in our own life? The answer to that question comes from an earlier chapter under the topic, the "born-again" experience. Salvation occurs through the desire to change and accept God's plan for salvation through Christ. Notice that there are no works involved. To do anything in the flesh in order to generate salvation is man's way of saying, "I did it myself." Only a surrender to Christ can produce salvation.

- Are ye so foolish? having begun in the Spirit, are ye now made perfect by the flesh? - (Galatians 3:3)

When we invite Jesus to be our Lord, we are saying, "No longer do I want sin to have dominion over me." This decision insures that the barriers of *sin, hell* and *death are* replaced with *grace, heaven* and *life.* The penalty of sin is paid in full and covered under the **blood of Christ**. In the same way, we can rest assured that the promises of God belong to us. "For all the promises of God in Him *are* yea, and in Him Amen..." 2 Corinthians 1:20.

- ...and the **blood of Jesus Christ** His Son cleanseth us from all sin. - (1 John 1:7)

Sowing to the Flesh:

Now let us take a look at how much influence the attributes of the flesh have on man. Mainly, the thoughts and concerns of man are attracted toward the flesh. The flesh becomes the important element of man, and consequently, a hindrance in the individual receiving salvation. As a rule, we want to keep the flesh in the best operating condition possible, so therefore, we devote much time at achieving that goal. Yes, we use the flesh for many of life's endeavors; however, Jesus said, "It is the spirit that quickeneth; the flesh profiteth nothing" John 6:63. The writer of Ecclesiastes issued this piece of advice:

- Whatsoever thy hand findeth to do, do *it* with thy might; for *there is* no work, nor device, nor knowledge, nor wisdom, in the grave, wither thou goest. - (Ecclesiastes 9:10)

We must recognize that the flesh is truly void of any advantages in consideration of the grave. Still, the writer of Ecclesiastes made another notable comment when he summarized his findings on life. After checking out the things done under the sun, he concluded with these three words; "all is vanity." The following Scriptures add to those findings regarding the flesh:

- For if ye live after the flesh, ye shall die: but if ye through the Spirit do mortify the deeds of the body, ye shall live. - (Romans 8:13)

- For he that soweth to his flesh shall of the flesh reap corruption; but he that soweth to the Spirit shall of the Spirit reap life everlasting. - (Galatians 6:8)

Seeking After Life:

One thing to keep in mind concerning the flesh and the spirit of man—the flesh is drawn to Satan and sin, while the spirit seeks after God and righteousness. Even without salvation, the natural instinct of the soul is to seek after the spirit where life originated. However, if the spirit is without life, the soul seeks after anything that seems to have life in it.

Although the soul instinctively knows that life comes from the spirit, it sees the flesh communicating the only life available within its being. Consequently, it uses the flesh as a substitute to fulfill its desires. Whatever our pleasure is in life, if it comes from the flesh, it yields only temporary pleasure. Not only that—the flesh itself is only temporary.

The Soul Seeks for Life:

The soul is conscious of the fact that the spirit is where real life originates. Accordingly, it seeks after life from the spirit through religions, good works, or just attempting to be good. Yet, even though the soul feels good about performing these deeds, the void still exists because the spirit is dead. As a result, without the Spirit of God attached to the spirit of man, he will continue to seek after life, but to no avail.

Two Types of Life:

To get an idea of the differences between an unsaved and a saved individual, we have outlined both illustrations. When mortal man dies, the blood, which is the life of the flesh, ceases its flow. The blood no longer is the life support system to keep him alive. Obviously, he does not take his earthly body with him to his final destination, but he does take his soul. Now let's take a look at these two individuals.

Unsaved Man: The following developments illustrate the results of an individual who dies without salvation. As indicated, the bloodflow ceases, which results in the elimination of life in the flesh. In addition, because he or she did not receive salvation while the opportunity existed, the union of his spirit to God's Spirit never occurred. Therefore, the soul never received life from the spirit. Subsequently, he has no life within himself, which can only mean that he is dead in his sins. So, when he departs from his body, his soul sets off for his new destination and his new home—the place described in the Bible as hell. This is the place where the individual selected as his choice to spend eternity.

Early in our studies we determined that God created man as an eternal being. Man became a living soul when God breathed into his nostrils. This living soul, although without the spirit, is still capable of receiving all the agony and pain hell can give.

Saved Man: In a related way, when a person dies, and he or she has accepted the salvation provided through Jesus Christ, a different situation occurs. As before, the life of the blood no longer responds in the individual because he or she is dead. However, this time, only the physical component of the individual dies. By reason of salvation, the eternal soul of this individual has life. This life comes from the fact that the spirit of man is reconnected to the Spirit of God. In this case, when he departs from his body, his soul sets off for his new destination and home—a place the Bible calls heaven.

In his earthly life, the "born-again" man continues to keep his body alive by the blood, but the Spirit of God keeps his soul and spirit alive. In this way, all the promises that the Bible makes regarding salvation belong to him including the assurance of eternal life. The following passage illustrates the condition of his flesh in contrast to his soul.

- ...but though our outward man perish, yet the inward *man* is renewed day by day. - (2 Corinthians 4:16)

The Deciding Factor:

Does the living soul tend to seek after life from the spirit or life from the flesh? When we answer this question, we also answer the question regarding salvation. The deciding factor of salvation depends on the choice worked out by the individual. Does he choose to accept the sacrifice Jesus paid for sin and receive Him as Lord and Savior, or does the individual reject Christ and choose to stay with Satan? Ultimately, whatever choice the individual makes determines his final destiny.

At Salvation—No Longer Earthly:

At salvation, the Spirit of God sends life into the soul of man. Although he once was dead, he is now alive. Hence, the individual is "born-again." The body is not "born-again," but the immaterial substances (the spirit and soul) are. Once the person's house of clay dies, the spirit and soul depart to be with the Lord Jesus so that 'where He is, there we may be also.'

The result of salvation rests in the fact that the individual no longer belongs to the earth but is born from above. Adam was made of an earthly substance. Thus, he belonged to the earth. Even after the fall of man, his soul was destined for the lower regions of the earth below. However, that all changed with salvation. Jesus was made of a heavenly substance and belongs to heaven. When we transfer our allegiance to Christ, we also transfer our residence.

False Prophets:

Jesus said, "Beware of false prophets, which come to you in sheeps clothing, but inwardly they are ravening wolves. You shall know them by their fruit..." Matthew 7:15,16. The apostle Paul points out that if there was another way back to God, then Christ died in vain.

Concerning the Biblical viewpoint, it remains clear that there is only one way back to God. Jesus said, "I Am the Way, the Truth and the Life, no man can come to the Father but by Me." Again it is written, "We must all work out our own salvation with fear and trembling." When considering the consequences, salvation looks like a sensible option.

Man Retained a Head Knowledge:

With heart knowledge removed, man retained a head knowledge of the Spirit of God after the fall. That makes this statement by Jesus worthy of note. "No man can come to Me, except the Father which hath sent Me draw him: and I will raise him up at the last day" John 6:44. Obviously, the Father will not disrupt the free will of man, but only by the stimulating of our spirit by the Father can one come to Jesus.

How does the Father know to draw a person to Jesus?

With only head knowledge of God remaining, the Spirit of God cannot penetrate and reconnect to the spirit of man. Yet, the Spirit of God is mindful of a man's desire for salvation.

The book of Proverbs provides this disclosure, "The spirit of man *is* the candle of the LORD, searching all the inward parts of the belly" Proverbs 20:27. The spirit of man is the candle, and the belly refers to the soul. In this way, God is able to know the heart of man by searching for signs of a desire to be saved.

Another way the Father uses to draw someone to Jesus is through the prayers of "born-again" individuals. "...The effectual fervent prayer of a righteous man availeth much" James 5:6. Prayer is a way God made for man to accomplish His work on earth.

When we pray for an individual to receive salvation, the Father works to draw that one to Jesus. When that individual finally receives salvation, Jesus sends the Holy Spirit to that one. Hence, we see the following:

The Father draws the individual to the Son. The Son sends forth His Holy Spirit. The Holy Spirit, now living in the individual, points the individual to Jesus and Jesus reveals the Father to the individual. Therein is the Godhead at work within man.

God Desires Salvation for All Men:

How does God feel about someone rejecting salvation? The following Scriptures give us an idea:

- Have I any pleasure at all that the wicked should die? saith the Lord God: *and* not that he should return from his ways, and live? - (Ezekiel 18:23)

- ...when the wicked *man* turneth away from his wickedness that he hath committed, and doeth that which is lawful and right, he shall save his soul alive. - (Ezekiel 18:27)

- For God sent not His Son into the world to condemn the world; but that the world through Him might be saved. - (John 3:17)

Summary of Chapter Eight:

The purpose of the Trinity is to make salvation available to mankind. This chapter pinpointed some of the details surrounding salvation. The cross did not automatically impart salvation to the human race. To do so would take back man's free-will. Man retained the knowledge of right and wrong, permitting him to decide if he wishes to accept God's free gift of eternal life.

The cross became our shortcut back to God. Instead of following our ancestry all the way back to Adam, where it is blocked from getting through to God, we now have direct access to God through Jesus Christ. The shortcut is activated when the individual receives salvation. His new simplified ancestry extends from the Holy Ghost, to Jesus to the Father.

An individual must take the first step toward redemption. Man had the choice to go from God to sin; man now has the choice to go from sin back to God. In so doing, his name is blotted out of Satan's "book of death," and written in the Lamb's "Book of Life."

Chapter 9

The Humanity Of Christ

Trinity and Life:

As you can see, there is a coherent relationship between life and the Trinity. More significantly, the availability of life could only come from one Source. Man traded life for death through disobedience to God. However, God created a way to restore that life by becoming incarnate in the second Person of the Trinity. At one point in time, man was without hope of life, but now eternal life is readily available through Jesus Christ because of Calvary's cross. How does the cross of 2000 years ago continue to bring salvation to man? The answer to that question is the intended focal point of this chapter.

The Ascension in Bodily Form:

Here we want to look at a couple of issues, allowing each one to expand our understanding of the Trinity. The first matter involves the ascension of Jesus Christ into heaven. For a closer view of this incident, we must turn our attention to one specific verse of Scripture. In this passage, we find that Jesus has scarcely finished issuing His final instructions to the apostles before He ascended into heaven. The Bible gives us a stunning picture of this dramatic event as it unfolded.

- And when He had spoken these things, while they beheld, He was taken up; and a cloud received Him out of their sight. - (Acts 1:9)

They Beheld Him Go Up:
We find something of specific interest within this verse of Scripture. When Jesus ascended into heaven, they beheld Him being taken up, disclosing that He went up in Body, Soul and Spirit. You ask, why is this important? Simply this: because the apostles watched as Jesus was taken up out of their sight reveals that Jesus ascended in His bodily form. Furthermore, if Jesus had assumed His deified position as God, salvation for humanity would be rendered as invalid. Perhaps we can secure a better grip on this observation by considering the following:

Dust to Dust:
In the book of Hebrews we find the following statement:

- And as it is appointed unto men once to die, but after this the judgment. - (Hebrews 9:27)

And, in the book of Genesis, God told Adam and Eve before their banishment from the Garden of Eden:

- In the sweat of thy face shalt thou eat bread, till thou return unto the ground; for out of it wast thou taken: for dust thou art, and unto dust shalt thou return. - (Genesis 3:19)

In view of Hebrews 9:27, we discover that man dies only once. As a Man, Jesus was subject to all the laws pertaining to man. He could only die once for our sins. Thus, there could not have been a second chance for the redemption of man.

The second Scripture, Genesis 3:19, takes note that the body of man returns to the dust of the ground, yet the soul of man, as established, goes to the place where destined. Although the body of Jesus was in human form, it did not return to the dust of the ground because it was not created from the dust of the ground. Jesus was born directly from God and could not "return to dust." For that reason, as happens with mortal man, His body returned to where it came from—the only difference is, His body came from heaven.

Flesh and Blood Cannot Enter Into Heaven:

Turning now to another passage of interest, we make this discovery, "Now this I say, brethren, that flesh and blood cannot inherit the kingdom of God; neither doth corruption inherit incorruption" 1 Corinthians 15:50.

Notice that flesh and blood cannot inherit the kingdom of God. Also observe here that it does not say flesh **or** blood, but flesh **and** blood. It helps to be aware of this detail as we take a look at some of the events that transpired after the resurrection of Christ. Bear in mind, our aim is to illustrate why and how Jesus, even to this day, remains in a human form. Certainly, it is a glorified human form, but nonetheless fashioned of a living Human Being.

Why is this important? Remember, God could not redeem man from His divine position. If Jesus had reclaimed His divinity, which He employed before His incarnation, His redemption efforts would have been in vain. The door of salvation would have closed for humanity. On the other hand, by ascending into heaven Body, Soul, and Spirit, Jesus was able to retain His status of a Man. Therefore, salvation, even now, remains in effect by way of a sinless Human Being. To further comprehend, let's explore some passages regarding Christ's humanity, both before and after His ascension into heaven.

Jesus Retained His Deity:

Our first impression might be that Jesus had to relinquish his divinity. Absolutely not. He continued to maintain His divinity after the crucifixion in the same fashion as before the crucifixion. The only time separation between the Father and the Son seemed to occur was when Jesus took upon Himself the sins of humanity. Just the same, when Jesus cried out, "My God, My God, why hast Thou forsaken Me?" separation did not truly occur. In spite of all appearances, it was not Jesus that the Father turned away from, but the sins.

- For as the Father hath life in Himself; so hath He given to the Son to have life in Himself; - (John 5:26)

If the Father had abandoned the Son, Jesus would still have had Life within Himself. That was the promise given to Him by the Father. Still, this marked the first time the Father could not behold the Son. We may perceive it in this manner—the attachment was there, but not the embrace. Once the sins were deposited and the penalty paid, the embrace returned again.

One of the most important details concerning the cross took place when Jesus cried out, "My God, My God, why hast Thou forsaken Me?" Matthew 27:46. Again we find this Scripture, but this time in the 22nd Psalm, which adds, "...*why art Thou so far from helping Me, and from* the words of My roaring?" No wonder Satan thought he had won the victory, but he could not outsmart God. Jesus could not have died unless He had sin.

Sin and the Innocent Man:
Jesus, a sinless being, was incapable of dying without the stain of sin. Death had no hold on Him since He was an innocent Man. However, that all changed at the cross. As it happened, He took the sins of the whole world upon Himself at Calvary.

Astoundingly, we find out it was the Father's good pleasure to bruise Him in order to redeem fallen man. Moreover, Jesus, in receiving those sins, marked the first time He became eligible to die. In reality, He took our punishment and died in our place.

Given that He was an innocent Man (that is, He never sinned in His own right), He could take those sins to the lower reaches of hell. For that reason, he was able to free the righteous beings held captive, and recover the keys of hell and of death.

- By which also He went and preached unto the spirits in prison; - (1 Peter 3:19)

- I am He that liveth, and was dead; and, behold, I am alive for evermore, Amen; and have the keys of hell and of death. - (Revelation 1:18)

Jesus Appears to His Disciples:

Let's look now at another event that took place right after the resurrection. We find the disciples gathered together, talking about Jesus, and how He had appeared to some of them.

- And as they thus spake, Jesus Himself stood in the midst of them, and saith unto them, Peace *be* unto you. But they were terrified and affrighted, and supposed that they had seen a spirit. And He said unto them, Why are ye troubled? and why do thoughts arise in your hearts? Behold My hands and My feet, that it is I Myself: handle Me, and see; for a spirit hath not flesh and bones, as ye see Me have. And when He had thus spoken, He showed them *His* hands and *His* feet. And while they yet believed not for joy, and wondered, He said unto them, Have ye here any meat? And they gave Him a piece of a broiled fish, and of an honeycomb. And He took *it*, and did eat before them. - (Luke 24:36-43)

In this passage, evidently Jesus was in a bodily form when He visited the disciples. There is no reason to doubt that the blood of Jesus spilled out at Calvary. The holes in His hands, feet and side no longer issued any more blood. Consequently, it would be sufficient for us to say that Jesus no longer had any blood in

His body. This agrees with the report from Luke 24:36-43 where Jesus reveals that He was not a spirit, and that He did have flesh and bone.

When we couple this discovery with His ascension, where His disciples watched Him go up, there can be no question that Jesus exists at this present time in a glorified human body. Since He is also God, the Spirit of God originates in Him. Consequently, He has life in Himself and does not need blood to sustain Him as we do for our mortal bodies.

Added Justification:
To justify our findings, there is one more Scripture in need of consideration. In 1 Timothy 2:5 we find this piece of evidence, "For there is one God, and one mediator between God and men, the Man Christ Jesus." The context of this verse reinforces what Jesus said in John 14:6, "…no man cometh unto the Father, but by Me." As plainly stated, Jesus is presently the only mediator between God and men. Not only that, but He is referred to as the Man, Christ Jesus. If He had ascended into heaven with just His Soul and His Spirit, He would exist only in His deified nature. Now He exists as earthly man does.

Keep in mind that only *sinless Man* could redeem *sinful man*. Jesus, by retaining His humanity, after His resurrection and ascension, gave mankind the certainty that salvation remains available for everyone. Even to this day. Jesus continues as the sinless Human Being, seated in heaven at the right hand of the Father. He is the only mediator between God and man, and the only way to God the Father.

The Disciples, the Great Commission and the Promises:
After Jesus ascended into heaven, His disciples were the ones left to carry on the work of announcing the Good News. For nearly three years the apostles and many disciples followed

Jesus. They watched, they listened and they learned all the things He said and did. They obtained everything they needed to know concerning the aspects of God and His Kingdom.

To make sure that they understood who He was, Jesus revealed Himself to them after His resurrection. By seeing and talking to Jesus they received encouragement to set the Great Commission as their number one priority. Man must become aware that redemption exists and know how to receive it.

Jesus did His part—now it was up to His followers to spread the news. Seeing Jesus in the flesh after the resurrection caused them to know the truth that He was the Son of God. Not only were they taught firsthand, but also Jesus promised to send to them the Holy Spirit after He ascended into heaven.

Ten days after the disciples watched Jesus go up into heaven the Holy Spirit came upon them in an upper room in Jerusalem. There they were all filled with the Holy Ghost fulfilling the promise Jesus made. Yet, there was one other promise Jesus made before He left this earth. He assured us that He would return for us, so that where He is, there we may be also.

- In My Father's house are many mansions: if it were not so, I would have told you. I go to prepare a place for you. - (John 14:2)
- And if I go and prepare a place for you, I will come again, and receive you unto Myself; that where I am, there ye may be also. - (John 14:3)

Blood in Heaven:

Now let us explore one more thing of relevance. In this chapter, references were made concerning two particular passages—one regarding flesh and bone, the other, flesh and blood. As was established, Jesus is in heaven with a Body made up of flesh and bone. The other passage, 1 Corinthians 15:50, assures us that flesh and blood cannot be in heaven. The question is, "Because flesh is in heaven, does that mean there is no blood in heaven?" In all probability, that would be the expected conclusion. But as it happened, according to one verse of Scripture, blood alone, apart from the flesh, does exist in heaven. The following passage illustrates this:

- ...heaven opened, and behold a white horse; and He that sat upon him was called Faithful and True, and in righteousness He doth judge and make war. - (Revelation 19:11)
- His eyes were as a flame of fire, and on His head were many crowns; and He had a name written, that no man knew, but He Himself. - (Revelation 19:12)
- And He was clothed with a vesture dipped in **blood**: and His name is called The Word of God. - (Revelation 19:13)

This passage makes for an interesting side-note with respect to what we have studied thus far. Although blood is found in heaven, it is not located within the flesh, but upon the vesture of Jesus Christ. Obviously, this is the same blood that Jesus shed for man at the cross. With good cause this blood would be allowed in heaven, since it is not stained by sin as contrasted with the contaminated, sin-infected blood of mortal man.

There is another slant to these three verses of Scripture (Revelation 19:11-13). Illustrated for us here is a picture of Jesus, ready to return to earth as King of kings and Lord of lords. This Scripture points out the Second Coming of the Lord to this earth. In reality, this is also the place in time where the religious leaders, who misread the Scriptures, were looking for their Messiah. What they neglected to foresee was the need of a Savior. In doing so, they ignored the necessity for salvation from the bondage of sin.

The Nail Prints:

The denial of Jesus as the Messiah has been handed down from generation to generation. Even though the rejection persists to this day, one must only turn to the Old Testament for verification of truth. Because Jesus ascended bodily into heaven, the nail prints are still visible in His body. Looking again to the 22nd Psalm we find the following:

- For dogs have compassed Me: the assembly of the wicked have enclosed Me: **they have pierced My hands and My feet**. - (Psalm 22:16)

Much of the 22nd Psalm is a picture of Jesus crucified on the cross. The above passage clearly indicates the nail prints from His crucifixion. Other Scripture passages regarding the wounds of the Messiah are found in the Book of Zechariah, however several Old Testament Books contain additional passages relating to the crucifixion.

- And I will pour upon the house of David, and upon the inhabitants of Jerusalem, the spirit of grace and of supplications: and they shall look upon **Me Whom they have pierced**, and they shall mourn for Him, as one mourneth for his only son, and shall be in bitterness for him, as one that is in bitterness for his first-born. - (Zechariah 12:10)

- And one shall say unto Him, What are these **wounds in Thine hands**? Then He shall answer, Those with which I was wounded in the house of My friends. - (Zechariah 13:6)

Not only do these passages provide an image of the Messiah Who was pierced and wounded, but also notice the second Person of the Trinity is speaking as God in Zechariah 12:10. This indicates that the Son of God existed before the incarnation occurred. The book of Revelation further notes, "Behold, He cometh with clouds; and every eye shall see Him, and they *also* which **pierced** Him: and all kindreds of the earth shall wail because of Him. Even so, Amen" Revelation 1:7.

The Humanity of Jesus in Heaven:

From our findings in this chapter we must conclude that Jesus does indeed reside in heaven at this present time. Furthermore, He exists in the same Body in which He ascended, made up of flesh and bone. The fact that His Body does not contain any blood justifies the Scripture, which declares flesh and blood cannot enter into heaven. Thus, our objective, confirming that Jesus is living in His human form, has been realized. It is clear: although His deity formulated our redemption, His humanity secured it. Nevertheless, He did not discard His deity to retain His humanity. Rather, even to this very day, He is fully God and fully Man, and because He is fully Man, His nail scarred hands and feet are visible today in heaven.

Summary of Chapter Nine:

The intent of this chapter was to illustrate the importance of the bodily ascension of Jesus into heaven. For Him to have left His humanity here on earth would have nullified redemption for mankind. Without the availability of the perfect Human Being, there could be no salvation available. The perfect Human Being must continue to be available to deliver man from the consequences of sin.

When Jesus ascended into heaven, the apostles watched Him go up, indicating that He went up in Body, Soul and Spirit. The body of man must return to the dust of the ground from where it was formed; therefore, the body of man stays on earth at death. The Body of Jesus was not of an earthly substance. He was born of the Holy Ghost from heaven. Therefore, His Body went back to where it originated.

Chapter 10

Issues Surrounding the Trinity

Matters and Issues:

We have touched on a number of essential issues relating to the Trinity. Noticeably, the Trinity has an influence on many other areas of doctrine. For that reason, these other doctrines have also come under the same scrutiny as the Trinity. So much so in fact, they have become issues of debate in their own right. Understanding these other areas will help clear up much of the contention that surrounds the Trinity. Therefore, we want to devote much of this chapter studying some of these and other issues, particularly the ones that have caused difficulties.

Questions and Debates:

For 2000 years, since the first coming of Christ, many have engaged in an attempt to discredit the Scriptures and particularly the Trinity. As depicted in the sixth chapter of Ephesians, flesh and blood is not behind these efforts, but rulers of the darkness of this world. It is outside the natural reasoning of man to conceive of someone in the form of a Human Being, and yet, not of the lineage of Adam. To make matters even more inconceivable, that Human Being is also God. Therefore, those in conflict with the Trinity continually warn people that Jesus was not really Who He said He was. While they believe that Jesus did exist, they cannot accept the fact that He was also God. With those thoughts in mind, let's look at some of the difficulties expressed by those opposed to the Trinity.

The Dedicated Followers:

During the ministry of Jesus, Scriptures indicate He had many followers. At one time He preached to four thousand men plus women and children, while at another time five thousand men plus women and children. The final count in the upper room was 120, and all received the baptism of the Holy Ghost on the day of Pentecost. That same day nearly 3000 souls were added to the Church, as recorded in Acts 2:41.

In view of the number of followers, we must conclude that Jesus certainly attracted people. The apostles were men chosen by Christ to follow Him, while the disciples chose to follow Him. All the apostles of Christ, except Paul, who was later chosen, and many of Christ's disciples followed Him throughout His ministry. If Jesus were only a man, it is inconceivable that His apostles and disciples would be willing to lay down their lives for Him. Yet, we find it compelling that a great number of these followers of Christ were more than willing to died a martyr's death rather than deny Him.

There is no reason to believe that these men were willing to simply give up their lives for someone who may have deceived them. Remember that each of these men not only saw Jesus and the works that He had done, but they were "born-again" believers filled with the Holy Ghost.

Non-Christian Issues: At this point, we want to look at some of the issues presented by those opposed to the Trinity. While they may be sincere in their beliefs, much of the difficulty stems from the fact that only God can interpret His Word. The natural mind, without the Spirit of God, is unable to grasp the deep things of God. "But God hath revealed *them* unto us by His Spirit: for the Spirit searcheth all things, yea, the deep things of God" 1 Corinthians 2:10. The issue of the Trinity is perhaps the deepest of all the doctrines relating to God.

To begin with, we have identified the following Scripture as one of the focal points of confusion by many non-Christians. Here we find Jesus talking to a group of Jews who sought to persecute and slay Him because He healed a man on the Sabbath. We will take one verse of Scripture out of the thirty verses contained in the complete passage which Jesus delivered to answer the Jews' accusation. Surprisingly, the passage could also be aimed at the very people disputing the Trinity today.

The Voice and Shape of God:

• And the Father Himself, which hath sent me, hath borne witness of Me. Ye have neither heard His voice at any time, nor seen His shape. - (John 5:37)

From this one verse, many have justified a motive for the rejection of the Trinity. Although the reasoning seems valid, the argument centers on the rationale that Jesus could not have been God, since no one has ever heard God's voice nor seen His shape. Furthermore, this opinion theorizes that if Jesus was God, this Scripture is a contradiction. This argument is based on the fact that the people Jesus was speaking to in this verse actually heard Jesus (God) speaking, and they also saw His shape. Stated another way—Jesus Himself is relating this very Scripture about God, while at the same time the people are listening to Him and looking at Him. In view of this Scripture, how can Jesus also be God in the flesh?

This logic seems credible when first encountered, but, as we shall see, it is void of accurate understanding. Remember, Jesus was in a human form and in a physical body. God is a Spirit and is in heaven. Assuredly, Jesus was speaking the words of God. Despite that, His voice did not sound like the voice of God but the voice of the human form He inhabited. Likewise, His shape was not in Spirit form but like that of a Human Being. The book of Exodus gives us a picture of the voice of God:

111

- And all the people saw the thunderings, and the lightnings, and the noise of the trumpet, and the mountain smoking: and when the people saw *it*, they removed, and stood afar off. And they said unto Moses, Speak thou with us, and we will hear: but let not God speak with us, lest we die. - (Exodus 20:18,19)

We can conclude from this passage that God's voice is so overwhelming, just to hear it could cause death. The same applies to seeing God's shape as depicted in this next verse:

- And He said, Thou canst not see My face: for there shall no man see Me, and live. - (Exodus 33:20)

Yes, this is a portrait of God, but not in a human form, as is the case with Jesus. It is God in His Spirit form. In this passage, God permitted Moses to glance at His backside, but this was because Moses requested to look at Him. Nevertheless, Moses did not see God's face. There can be no doubt that the thunderous voice of the Father would frighten even the bravest human. To look upon God in His Spirit form would cause immediate death.

The Difficulty in Confirming His Deity:
Another notable hindrance to those who oppose the Trinity is this, "If Jesus was really God, why didn't He just come right out and say so?" This too sounds like a valid question until we consider the following observation. It is important to recognize that regardless if Jesus had told them time and again He was God, and, in spite of everything, confirmed His deity with great signs and miracles—what justification would it have produced to redeem man? Chances are they would not have crucified Christ, and thus, would have defeated the very purpose for His coming to earth. Again recall that it was His humanity and not His deity that produced salvation.

Jesus Performed Miracles and Healings:

On the other hand—didn't Jesus do many works of miracles, such as changing water into wine, raising the dead, and all manners of healings? To answer this question, we must also take into account that, at the time before His crucifixion, the full story had not been told. Even the apostles did not understand until after the resurrection, and even then, not completely. Only after the Holy Ghost fell upon them in the upper room were they aware of their calling. If they were following a man who claimed to be a prophet or someone who said he was sent by God, without any other evidence but his word, it would not have been wise, even by today's standards. There was something about Jesus that made these apostles leave everything they had and immediately follow Him.

So then, why did Jesus do the works that He did? Jesus answered this question Himself. He did them because, even if they did not believe on Him, they could believe for His work's sake. Bear in mind that if Jesus had not done *any* works, many even today would question His deity. However, we must also take into account that His followers were eyewitnesses to the works and saw them firsthand. Without these followers, what good would it have been to redeem man if no one else would know about it? For this reason, they saw, they believed, and they proclaimed the message of salvation throughout the land.

The Promise of the Holy Ghost:

Even more remarkable was the promise of the third Person of the Trinity. Remember, after the fall of man, the Holy Spirit never entered the heart of man in the Old Testament. The prophets of old were inspired and filled by the Holy Ghost with wisdom and knowledge. Nevertheless, only through redemption could their hearts be filled. Certainly, they were righteous men and used by God, but even they prophesied of the day when God *would* pour out His Spirit.

On the day of Pentecost, Peter gave this account, "But this is that which was spoken by the prophet Joel; And it shall come to pass in the last days, saith God, I will pour out of My Spirit upon all flesh..." Acts 2:16,17. Ezekiel reports this, "And I will put My Spirit within you..." Ezekiel 36:27.

Jesus assured us that He would send His Holy Spirit to those who accept Him as Lord. Jesus cannot be everywhere because He exists today in a human form. On the other hand, the Holy Spirit *is* omnipresent and available to every individual. Therefore, by the promise of the Holy Ghost we have the guarantee of our salvation.

Jesus—a Prophet Like Moses:
Let's look at one more difficult passage for non-Christians, this time from the Old Testament. Moses remarked to the Israelites that "The Lord thy God will raise up unto thee a Prophet from the midst of thee, of thy brethren, like unto me; unto Him ye shall hearken;" Deuteronomy 18:15. The contention here is that Moses was a man, and the Prophet to be raised up by God would be like Moses. Since Moses was only a mortal being, the Prophet would likewise be only a mortal being.

Accurately, Jesus was a Prophet like Moses, but He was not a man like Moses. Again, this rationale seems logical until we consider that the Israelites were slaves in Egypt and that Moses was the one who saved them. This is only a shadow of the Prophet Who was to come. As Moses led the Israelites from slavery through the wilderness and to *the promise land*, so Jesus leads us out of slavery to sin through this earthly journey to *the Promised Land*.

Christian Issues: Next we will take a look at some issues that have caused conflict in the Christian community. The first one is more an issue of controversy rather than an issue of doctrine.

Where Do Little Children and Babies Fit In?

A concern of many parents is that regarding their children. The question is that since man inherited the sin nature, are little children also condemned? Obviously, we must turn again to the Scriptures for the answer. Jesus pointed out several things pertaining to babies and small children. Notice here that the children we are talking about have yet to acquire the knowledge of good and evil. As a result, babies and children without this knowledge have not yet come under bondage to sin.

- But Jesus said, Suffer little children, and forbid them not, to come unto Me: for of such is the kingdom of heaven. - (Matthew 19:14)

Without the knowledge, little children are connected to God's Spirit and remain so until understanding comes to them. Notice, Jesus does not say children, but little children. Little children are more dependent upon their parents. As the parallel to this passage suggests, we should be more dependent upon God. In another passage, Jesus discloses an important lesson about the purity of children and the Kingdom of Heaven.

- Jesus said, Verily, I say unto you, Except ye be converted, and become as little children, ye shall not enter into the kingdom of heaven. - (Matthew 18:3)

The question to ask here is—would we want to become as little children if they are not saved? The little child does not have the stain of sin; therefore he is able to enter into the Kingdom of God. When the child reaches the age where he knows good from evil, he then becomes responsible for his actions. Remember; it is sin that keeps man out of heaven. A baby or a small child, although he has inherited the sin nature, does not have the awareness. Accordingly, he cannot be held responsible until that time when accountability is reached.

In the book of Romans, Paul gives this depiction of sin and the law. This is a picture of a child who does not know good from evil, which is the law.

- ...For without the law sin *was* dead. - (Romans 7:8)
- For I was alive without the law once: but when the commandment came, sin revived, and I died.- (Romans 7:9)

After the child reaches the point of accountability, the only way he can be set free from the stain of sin is by receiving the free gift of God through Jesus Christ. When this event occurs—no matter what the age—he essentially becomes as a little child again and one who is obedient to his Father. The nature of Christ replaces the nature of sin, and the person is eligible a second time to enter into the Kingdom of God, just as he was as a little child. In essence, he is "born-again."

Before the little child becomes accountable for his or her actions, the adult becomes answerable for the child. The gospel of Matthew furnishes us with the principle below. Interestingly, we find this passage has a double meaning. Not only does it refer to little children, but also to the ones who receive God's free gift of eternal life.

- And whoso shall receive one such little child in My name receiveth Me. - (Matthew 18:5)
- But whoso shall offend one of these little ones which believe in Me, it were better for him that a millstone were hanged around his neck, and *that* he were drowned in the depth of the sea. - (Matthew 18:6)

Notice here, this Scripture says that by merely offending a small child, or a believer of Christ, the consequences are dreadful. Thus, it would suffice us to keep this in mind when dealing with both types of children that believe in Him.

Mary and the Virgin Birth:

The following two issues have to do with matters of controversy within Christianity. Like the Trinity, the Virgin Birth has been a sensitive topic for many years. As mentioned, some churches reject the concept of the Virgin Birth altogether. Largely, these churches are of the same denominations that also reject the Trinity. The other area of question has to do with Mary, regarded by some as the mother of God. Since these two issues have a direct impact on the Trinity, we want to address them here with clear and simple reasoning.

Rejecting the Virgin Birth:

Perhaps a quick review of the Jewish wedding arrangements at the time of Jesus would be of help before we discuss the issue of the Virgin Birth.

The Jewish Wedding:

The Jewish wedding actually had two parts similar to the engagement of Western culture today. The first part consisted of creating the arrangements and agreement for the marriage after which the bridegroom went away to prepare a place in which to live. This is referred to as the espousal or betrothal period. By all rights the man and woman were married in the espousal interlude; however, the wedding ceremony still had to be performed. During the espousal period the bridegroom could divorce, but only because of infidelity. When the place to live in was ready, the bridegroom came back for the bride, which brings us to the second part. The second part involved the actual wedding ceremony after which time they lived together.

Situations Regarding the Virgin Birth:

Mary and Joseph were in the espousal period at the time the angel appeared to each of them separately. Therefore, they had no intimate contact at the time. Taking this into account, let's consider three cases regarding the Virgin Birth.

Virgin Birth and Situation Number One:

The first situation to consider is this—what if Mary had been a single woman and not a virgin? If Mary was single and not a virgin, according to biblical law, she would have been living in sin. Surely she would have been a harlot, and indeed, not a suitable instrument for God to use to bring forth His Son.

Virgin Birth and Situation Number Two:

Now, let's consider the second situation. What if Mary was a single woman and still a virgin? In this case, being with child of the Holy Ghost and single would again mark her as a harlot because she was single and yet with child.

Virgin Birth and Situation Number Three:

Let's take our third situation into account. Consider the occurring circumstances if Mary and Joseph would have had intimate contact before she was with child by the Holy Ghost. Certainly God could not use her in this case either, as He would be violating His own principle that He set down for mankind, "Thou shalt not commit adultery."

If Mary were not a virgin, it would nullify everything in the Old and New Testaments. Rejecting the Virgin Birth would signify Jesus was an offspring of Adam, and thus, Jesus Himself would be in need of salvation. As demonstrated, there can be no other explanation for the birth of Christ other than the Virgin Birth. As it turned out, God was right—Mary had to be a virgin to bring His plan of redemption into the world.

Mary, the Mother of God?

The next presumption to weigh is the topic of Mary, revered by some as the mother of God. Considering Who God is and His longevity, it pales to warrant any mortal being from the lineage of Adam and from the dust of the ground to be God's mother. Yet, this is the belief many were taught from childhood.

We have already noted how the Redeemer came to earth as a Human Being through the virgin Mary. Certainly there were other virgins available at the time Mary was chosen. Still and all, she was of the right family tree, and at the proper time Scripture was fulfilled. Mary was the instrument God employed to bring His Son into the world.

Needless to say, she raised Jesus and kept Him until He was ready to be on His own. She did everything that was expected of a mother in raising a child; nevertheless, Mary did not remain a virgin after the birth of Jesus. Mary and Joseph were married for at least twelve years, and it is told in the Scriptures that when Jesus was twelve years of age, they went looking for Him, and found Him in the temple.

Truly, Mary and Joseph would not have lasted through twelve years of marriage without physical intimacy, and if intimacy did occur, Mary would no longer be a virgin. The fact is, the Bible reports that Jesus had several brothers and sisters, and the names of the brothers are mentioned (Matthew 12:46; Matthew 13:55; Mark 6:3; Luke 8:19; John 2:12; Acts 1:14).

Without question, Mary was a blessed woman and is deserving of honor for being the one chosen as the mother of Jesus. Still, we must ask, was she really the mother of God? Certainly, she was the mother of His humanity; however, nowhere in Scripture is found where Jesus called Mary His mother—He referred to her as woman.

Did Mary, whose genealogy extends back to Adam, as recorded in the gospel, truly give birth to God? If she was an offspring of Adam, it stands to reason that she was in need of a Savior as much as we are. In actuality, she acknowledges her need for a Savior in the gospel of Luke 1:47, "And my spirit hath rejoiced in God my Saviour."

So then, is it wrong to believe Mary to be the mother of God? No, even some scholars cannot give a suitable explanation. Where the danger exists is in the worship of Mary. Scripture is clear—worship belongs to God alone.

The Issue of Sin:
We have referred to sin many times in our study. What has sin to do with the Trinity? Everything, considering that sin initiated the need *for* the Trinity.

What is sin? The Bible describes it as the transgression of the law (1 John 3:4). We conclude from Scripture that all have sinned and come short of the glory of God (Romans 3:23). The Bible also indicates there are no differences in transgression.

- For whosoever shall keep the whole law, and yet offend in one *point*, he is guilty of all. - (James 2:10)
- For He that said, Do not commit adultery, said also, Do not kill. Now if thou commit no adultery, yet if thou kill, thou art become a transgressor of the law. - (James 2:11)

- If we say that we have no sin, we deceive ourselves, and the truth is not in us. - (1 John 1:8)
- If we confess our sins, He is faithful and just to forgive us *our* sins, and to cleanse us from all unrighteousness. - (1 John 1:9)

The soul of the *natural man* is stained by sin. Certainly, some are more stained than others, but all are stained. As Adam and Eve gave in to sin, so each person shall venture through the same process. The following verse is a portrait of salvation:

- ... let us reason together, saith the LORD: though your sins be as scarlet, they shall be as white as snow; though they be red like crimson, they shall be as wool. - (Isaiah 1:18)

One who has never encountered *the new birth*, has never had his sins placed under the blood of Jesus. His only quality is his sin-nature, which operates from the flesh. The only way to rid the soul of the stain of sin is by washing it in the blood of Jesus.

For one who has experienced *the new birth*, the Scriptures specify that the blood of Jesus covers his sins. Is this to say God does not love the sinner? When we understand that the actual reason for the cross was to save sinners, that question is without merit. God loves man period. Good, or bad, He still loves us. The question might be; does the sinner love God?

Summary of Chapter Ten:

Many questions and debates have occurred over the years regarding the Trinity. One major question is this, "If Jesus was God, why didn't He just come out and announce it?" Another question becomes, "Why then did He do all the miracles and healings if He did not want anyone to know that He was, in fact, God in the flesh?"

These are some of the questions used to discredit the Trinity. The accusations generally are the results of misunderstanding of the true purpose and reason for the Trinity. Nevertheless, untold hours are spent by individuals in a mission to distort the Scriptures. However, all this time could be saved by taking a minute to invite Jesus into their lives.

Some of the Christian difficulties addressed in this chapter concerned the Virgin Birth, and Mary, regarded by some as the mother of God. These two hindrances will no longer be an issue when we resolve the mystery associated with the Trinity.

Chapter 11

Life, Offices and Names

The Characteristics of God:
The Old and New Testaments, clearly recognize God as one God. At the same time, the Trinity declares there to be three distinct but related entities. When we compared the make-up of man, as presented in an earlier chapter, with the structure of the Trinity, we saw a resemblance between the two.

It will help, at this point, to take another glance at man's structure. As we noted earlier, man's spirit is the conduit for the Spirit of God to flow into and fill his soul with life. His soul encases the intelligence and is the invisible body made in the likeness of God. The physical body is for recognition by others as well as performing physical duties while alive upon the earth. As you can see, there are not three men doing different things, but one man with three distinct, yet related entities.

In like manner, God's three entities also perform different tasks even though they are One. They too have a common agreement existing within the separate entities. For instance, God is the source of all life, and, while that designation applies to the Father, it applies also to the Son and to the Holy Ghost. Throughout the Bible we can find valuable insight into the structure and characteristics of God and how those characteristics operate. In this chapter, we want to look at some of these passages along with words pertaining to life.

The Words of Life:

1.- *The Blood:*

The *blood* was presented in an earlier chapter as the life of the flesh. This is the blood as associated to man, but when used in connection with Jesus, the word "blood" takes on a totally different meaning. A statement by Jesus in the Gospel of John links His blood spiritually to man. What He reported in His statement caused many of His disciples to leave Him. Jesus said, "Whoso eateth My flesh, and drinketh My blood, hath eternal life; and I will raise him up at the last day" John 6:54.

Jesus was not talking about blood in a fleshly context but from a spiritual viewpoint because the flesh profits nothing; it is the spirit that quickens. Some contend that He is referring to the sacrament of Communion. Note here, those who eat His flesh and drink His blood have eternal life, and Jesus said He would raise them up at the last day. Only by way of the "born-again" experience is eternal life produced. Communion is a covenant confirmation of that acceptance. The blood shed by Christ on Calvary's cross covers the sins we have generated in our lives. "But if we walk in the light, as He is in the light, we have fellowship one with another, and the blood of Jesus Christ His Son cleanseth us from all sin" 1 John 1:7.

We Believe by Faith:

With our natural mind and sight, we tend to think of things as we see them in the physical world. However, the backdrop of the unseen world is faith. The Bible defines faith as: "...the substance of things hoped for, the evidence of things not seen" Hebrews 11:1. We cannot see the blood covering of Christ's shed blood, but to receive it, we must believe that it is there. That applies to everything about our affairs with the spirit world. Jesus said, "When you pray, believe that you receive and you shall have." Although we cannot see our prayers, we must believe they go up and God hears them and will answer.

The Fact of Faith:

To expound further on the fact of faith while keeping in mind the biblical definition, call to mind the illustration of the wire and the light switch from a previous chapter. We established that the light switch was in the "off" position because of sin. When we accept what Jesus did for us at Calvary, and believe in our heart that God raised Him from the dead, the light switch goes to the "on" position. As a result, the Spirit of God surges through the wire to the heart. This in turn produces a restoration of new life to replace the death that disobedience created. So, when the surge of this life-giving current flows into the heart, it results in an awareness of a changed heart and nature. In other words, faith is changed to reality.

By virtue of God's Spirit connecting to our spirit, the new birth experience allows a faith, which can be realized. Hence, the definition of faith as depicted in Hebrews 11:1 is verified. When the Spirit of God enters the heart of the individual, faith ceases to be faith. The key here is that when faith (the substance of things hoped for) becomes factual, it is no longer hoped for; thus, when hope is realized, so is faith.

Words of the Source of Life:

Even though the blood gives life to the flesh, yet that life still originates from God. In view of this, the Bible indicates there are other sources of life, yet, as we investigate further, we shall find they are really of the same source—God. With our discovery we also find that these sources of life are closely identified with our topic of the Trinity. As we have indicated from the beginning, the Trinity and life are inseparable. In this section, we shall take a look at the actual words connected to the Trinity that are described in the Scriptures to mean life. We already looked at the blood, which is the *life* for the flesh. Now we want to look at four other words that have the same meaning in Scripture as the word "life."

2.- *The Spirit:*

The second of our series of words meaning, "life," is **Spirit**. By the *Spirit* of God, everything else receives its *life*. The following are Scriptures connecting *Spirit* to *life*.

* For the law of the *Spirit of life* in Christ Jesus hath made me free from the law of sin and death. - (Romans 8:2)

* And if Christ *be* in you, the body is dead because of sin; but the *Spirit is life* because of righteousness. - (Romans 8:10)

* Who also hath made us able ministers of the new testament; not of the letter, but of the spirit: for the letter killeth, but the *spirit giveth life*. - (2 Corinthians 3:6)

These passages provide three different approaches connecting the word *Spirit* to *life*. Hence, we find the *Spirit of life*, the *Spirit is life*, and the *spirit giveth life*. All excerpts are in agreement. Also notice the connection of the second and third Persons of the Trinity, (Christ Jesus and the Spirit).

3.- *The Word:*

The word **Word** also indicates *life* as presented in the Scriptures. Here are some Scriptures linking *Word* to *life*.

* Verily, verily I say unto you, He that heareth My *word*, and believeth on Him who sent Me, hath everlasting *life*, and shall not come into condemnation; but is passed from death unto life. - (John 5:24)

In the above verse Jesus makes the connection that hearing His *Word*, and believing on His Father shall give a person *life*. This indicates that just believing on the Father does not give eternal *life*, but the condition of hearing His *Word* is also required.

- That which was from the beginning, which we have heard, which we have seen with our eyes, which we have looked upon, and our hands have handled, of the *Word of life*; - (1 John 1:1)

In the above Scripture, John, who was one of the Twelve apostles, is categorically reporting his firsthand knowledge about Jesus, and calls Him the *Word of life*.

- ...the *words* that I speak unto you, *they* are *spirit*, and *they* are *life.* - (John 6:63)

In this last verse (John 6:63), Jesus advises us that His words are *Spirit* and they are *life.* Why are the words spoken by Him Spirit and life? Because Jesus is relaying the words God is giving Him through His human body. This also agrees with what our previous chapters have taught us. Jesus's words are not *Spirit* and *life* because they are merely words. They are *Spirit* and *life* because they are words that come from the Godhead whether it be the Father, the Son, or the Holy Spirit.

4.- *The Truth:*

The next word on our list is *Truth.* This word will come into better focus later on, but its importance in this verse of Scripture gives some indication of its real value.

- Jesus saith unto him, I am the Way, the *Truth*, and the *Life*: no man cometh unto the Father, but by Me. - (John 14:6)

5.- *Jesus:*

The last word we will look at is *Jesus.* As noted in the previous verse above, *Jesus* called Himself "*the Life.*" Notice He did not say I am "*a Life.*" By making this statement, Jesus is making Himself equal with God, who is the *Source of all life.* This is made evident in the next Scripture passage.

- For as the *Father* hath *life* in Himself; so hath He given to the *Son* to have *life* in Himself; - (John 5:26)

As noted earlier, *Jesus* is in heaven in a physical Body void of any *blood* to sustain Him. As God has *life* in Himself, so also *Jesus* has *life* in Himself, and that *life* sustains Him.

Connecting the Words:
These words have all indicated that they mean *life*. When we connect the words together, we shall see the meaning of each more clearly. Taking into account that the blood concerns both the flesh and the covering of sin, we will not make use of the blood for this part of the study. This is certainly not to deny the importance of the blood as it pertains to man. It was presented simply because it denotes life to both the body and the spirit. Now, let's examine the connections of the other four words.

Spirit, Word, Truth* and *Jesus:
What is the significance of finding these remaining four words which all mean life? Only this; if life comes from God alone, then *Jesus* who is *the Truth, the Life* and *the Word*, and the *Spirit* or *Holy Spirit* is also *the Life*, then there can be no question concerning both entities as God. The impact of these findings confirms the reality of the Trinity. These passages clearly reveal that these four words denote *life,* and there can be no doubt as to their meaning. In the following passages we see these words again, yet this time they are connected with one or more of the other words meaning *life*.

- In the beginning was the *Word* and the *Word* was with **God**, and the *Word* was **God**. - (John 1:1)

- ...the *Word* of the Lord in thy mouth is *Truth*. - (1 Kings 17:24)

- ...Thy *Word* is *Truth*. - (John 17:17)

- ...The sword of the *Spirit*, which is the *Word* of God: - (Ephesians 6:17)

- And I will pray the Father, and He shall give you another Comforter, that He may abide with you for ever; - (John 14:16)
- Even the *Spirit* of *Truth*; whom the world cannot receive, because it seeth Him not, neither knoweth Him: but ye know Him; for He dwelleth with you, and shall be in you. - (John 14:17)
- I will not leave you comfortless: I will come to you. - (John 14:18)

These Scriptures present a clear tie-in with each word as it relates to *life*. In the last Scripture, John 14:16-18, *Jesus* prays that the Father will send another Comforter (*the Spirit of Truth*) to be with the disciples after His ascension. In verse 18, He makes it obvious that the *Spirit of Truth* is really *Jesus* Himself as He announces, "I will not leave you comfortless: I will come to you." This disclosure coupled with the statement of Jesus that "the Father and I are One," should leave no reservation as to the relationship of the Godhead.

In conclusion, we have established that the *Word* is *Life*, *Jesus* is *Life*, the *Spirit* is *Life*, the *Spirit* of *Truth* and the *Word* is *Truth*, therefore, *Truth* must also be *Life*. Since God is the source of all *life*, by connecting the four words, we find not only do they each stand for *life*, but also they each mean "*the Life*."

God is a Spirit:
Overall, when the Bible speaks of God, it talks of the Father. While Jesus was talking to the woman at the well, He presented us with a notable detail about the Father.

128

- But the hour cometh, and now is, when the true worshippers shall worship the Father in spirit and in truth: for the Father seeketh such to worship Him. - (John 4:23)
- God *is* a Spirit: and they that worship Him must worship *Him* in spirit and in truth. - (John 4:24)

Notice here that two of the four words, (*spirit* & *truth*) are used in this passage of Scripture. Furthermore, Jesus enlightens us to the fact that God is a Spirit. While we already knew this fact, it permits us to get a picture of Jesus becoming Man. Bear in mind that Jesus was the first-born of God, which meant that the Spirit of God was connected to the Spirit of Jesus. This is the same way the "born-again" man is connected directly to God as was disclosed in an earlier chapter. Nevertheless, this might confuse some because it looks as though there are two different spirits we are dealing with here. It must be pointed out that the Spirit of God, although able to dwell in the hearts of many, is nonetheless one Spirit. A representation of this can be found in the gospel of Matthew in the following passage:

But when they deliver you up, take no thought how or what ye shall speak: for it shall be given you in that same hour what ye shall speak. - (Matthew 10:19)
For it is not ye that speak, but the Spirit of your Father which speaketh in you. - (Matthew 10:20)

Obviously for the Spirit of the Father to speak in you and through you, you must first have the Spirit of God living in you. These Scriptures can only refer to those who have received the Spirit of God. Due to the plan of redemption, it is now possible for every man, woman and child to be restored to his intended state of fellowship with God. Of the many who have received salvation, each saved individual also received the Spirit of God. This renders a portrayal that the Spirit of God remains one Spirit. This is known as the omni-presence of God.

Names and Offices:

At this time we want to direct our study from life to some of t
offices employed by each Person of the Godhead. Th
information will help strengthen much of what we have alrea
accumulated regarding the Trinity. What we have listed here a
some of the names, which are attributed to either the Father, t
Son, or the Holy Ghost. However, you should also be aware th
some of the offices or names apply to only one member of t
Godhead, while others apply to two or all three.

Due to the number of Scriptures, only the references are list
here. Take a few minutes to read through some or all of the:
passages in order to better understand the distinctions ma
between each member. Let's take a look now at those pertainir
to the Father first.

Names and Offices of the Father:
*With the names or offices shown first and the Scriptur
references following, these are in relation to the offices of Go
the Father.*

Almighty ------ Genesis 17:1; Job 35:13; Psalms 91:1
Creator -------- Genesis 1:1; Isaiah 40:28; Romans 1:25
Father ---------- Psalms 68:5; Isaiah 63:16; Malachi 2:10
First and Last Isaiah 41:4; 44:6; 48:12
Jehovah -------- Exodus 6:3; Psalms 83:18; Isaiah 12:2
Judge ----------- Genesis 18:25; Isaiah 33:22; Hebrews 12:23
King ------------- Psalms 5:2; Isaiah 6:5; 1Timothy 1:17
Lord ------------- Psalms 18:31; Isaiah 42:8; Jeremiah 10:6
Preserver ------ Job 7:20; Psalms 121:8; Isaiah 49:8
Redeemer ------ Psalms 78:35; Isaiah 44:24; 54:8
Saviour --------- 2 Samuel 22:3; Isaiah 43:11; John 4:42

Names and Offices of the Son:
*The following list includes some of the names or offices of th
second Person of the Trinity.*

Anointed One---Luke 4:18; Acts 10:38
Creator --------- Ephesians 3:9; Colossians 1:16
Father ----------- Isaiah 9:6
First and Last - Revelations 1:17; 22:13
God -------------- Isaiah 9:6; John 20:28; Acts 7:59
Judge ------------ Acts 10:42; Romans 2:16; 2 Timothy 4:1
King ------------- Matthew 2:2; 1 Timothy 6:15
Lord ------------- Matthew 20:31; Romans 1:3; Galatians 6:14
Mighty God ---- Psalms 50:1; Isaiah 9:6; Jeremiah 32:18
Preserver ------- 2 Timothy 4:18
Redeemer ------- Job 19:25; Titus 2:14; Galatians 4:4
Saviour ---------- Luke 2:11; 2 Timothy 1:10; Titus 1:4
Son -------------- Psalms 2:7; Isaiah 9:6; Daniel 3:25

Names and Offices of the Holy Ghost:
The following are some of the names and tasks designated to the Holy Spirit.
Anointer -------- Isaiah 61:1; Luke 4:18; Acts 10:38
Baptist ---------- Matthew 3:11; Acts 1:5
Comforter ------ John 14:16; 14:26; 16:7
Father ----------- Matthew 10:20; Luke 11:13; John 15:26
Fruits of Spirit Galatians 5:22,23
Giver of Gifts --1 Corinthians 12:7-11
God -------------- Genesis 1:2; Matthew 3:16; Acts 5:3,4
Sanctifier ------- Romans 15:16; 1 Corinthians 6:11
Teacher --------- John 14:26; 1 John 2:27

Notice that some offices are shared with *all members* of the Godhead, while others are shared with *one other member*. Still, some titles are unique to *only one member* of the Godhead.

Designated Offices:
In this section, we want to look at the Scriptures relating to some of those designated offices that are shared with more than one member of the Godhead.

Creator the Father:

- ...the everlasting God. the LORD, the **Creator** of the ends of the earth, fainteth not, neither is weary.... - (Isaiah 40:28)

Creator the Son:

- For by Him were all things created, that are in heaven, and that are in earth, visible and invisible, whether ... thrones, or dominions, or principalities, or powers: all things were **created** by Him, and for Him: - (Colossians 1:16)

God (Referring to the Father):

- He shall cry unto Me, Thou art my Father, my God, and the Rock of my salvation. - (Psalms 89:26)

God (Referring to the Son):

- And they stoned Stephen, calling upon *God*, and saying, Lord Jesus, receive my spirit. - (Acts 7:59)

God (Referring to the Holy Spirit):

- But Peter said, Ananias, why hath Satan filled thine heart to lie to the Holy Ghost.... - (Acts 5:3)
- ...why hast thou conceived this thing in thine heart? thou hast not lied unto men, but unto God. - (Acts 5:4)

We find that some of the offices designated for the Father are also relevant for the Son and the Holy Spirit. Thus, various names and offices pertaining to the Trinity are interchangeable. The significance of these Scriptures is purely for reference purposes to demonstrate that God is not separated into three different people. His entire being is a multiple of one; however, like man, God is composed of a triune entity.

Summary of Chapter Eleven:

The aim of this chapter was to introduce you to other ways to recognize the unified existence of the Godhead. So, by accumulating and establishing the validity of the Trinity, it will be easier to see how God can exist in three Persons.

Chapter 12

Prophecies of the Messiah

Where Difficulty Exists:
Where does the biggest difficulty lie regarding the Trinity? In all probability, it has to do with God the Son. We must conclude that if the Trinity consisted of only the Father and the Holy Ghost, there would be no mystery. Of course, there would be no salvation either. For that reason, most of our study and attention has centered on the second Person of the Trinity.

Thus far we have looked at several Scripture references relating to the life of Christ on earth. In this chapter, we want to further focus on Jesus by looking at some Old Testament prophecies relating to the first coming. These additional details will aid in reinforcing evidence from previous chapters. It will also paint a portrait of how the Father's plan of redemption originated.

Abraham, Israel and Jesus:
Genesis 3:8 hints that God walked with man in "the Garden," but after man's disobedience, the walks ended. After that, God's focus presumably centered on the redemption of man. To reach this objective, God raised up a man named Abraham. When he was one hundred years old, a son named Isaac was born to Abraham and his wife Sarah, fulfilling the promise of God. By faith—believing God is true, Abraham was willing to sacrifice his son Isaac. God prevented the sacrifice, but this faith was to become the basis of salvation for all mankind.

Through Abraham, his son Isaac, and Isaac's son Jacob, God established a covenant. In this way the nation of Israel was birthed. Israel became the apple of God's eye and His chosen people. After becoming slaves in Egypt, God sent a man named Moses to set his people free from their bondage. During this time, God gave Moses "the Ten Commandments." Throughout the history of the Jewish people, there have been times of obedience and times of rebellion toward God. For the most part God displayed compassion toward them.

Overlooked—the Need for a Savior:
Scattered throughout the Holy Scriptures were the promises of a Messiah (Redeemer), yet confusion existed because the Savior was to come to earth twice. Some of the leaders among the Jewish people only perceived the Second Coming of the Messiah. Many did not fully understand the need for a Savior.

When the Savior finally arrived, word of His ministry spread rapidly. Within a short time, He had many followers. Nevertheless, after His ministry took hold, many came to realize that the message He presented was different from that taught by the religious leaders.

A Scripture passage taken from the gospel of John provides this illustration: Jesus was talking to a certain group concerning the death He was to experience. He said to them, "And I, if I be lifted up from the earth, will draw all *men* unto Me. This He said, signifying what death He should die. The people answered Him, We have heard out of the law that Christ abideth for ever: and how sayest Thou, The Son of man must be lifted up? who is this Son of man?" John 12:32-34

They heard that the Messiah was to come, and when He did come He would abide forever. What they failed to realize was that He must first come to redeem fallen humanity.

The Scheme Seemed Right:

This had to make Satan happy, since it fit right into his scheme. On the other hand, it also fit into the design of an all-knowing God. Jesus could not have assumed our place at death unless He paid the full price for our redemption. Therefore, when Christ was crucified, the religious leaders were happy because Jesus quit preaching against their doctrine. Satan was happy until he realized what he had done by killing an innocent Man. God was also happy, but it must have hurt Him deeply to see it happen. However, the success of Calvary more than made up for the suffering it caused because the children of God were restored into right fellowship once again.

Guilt and Denial:

Another difficulty appeared because of what happened at "Calvary." The crucifixion of an innocent man, not only won our release, but it also placed a guilt trip on the Jewish people. Because of this rejection of Jesus as the Messiah, God made salvation available to the non-Jewish (Gentile) people as well. The result—many Jews and Gentiles alike have come to receive God's gift of eternal life. This extension of salvation to all men has become known as "the Dispensation of Grace."

Old Testament Prophecies:

The Old Testament contains many prophecies of the coming Messiah. Every prophecy connected to His first coming was fulfilled in Jesus. At this point, we want to look at some of those Old Testament prophecies. The fact that all of the ones relating to the first coming of Christ were fulfilled in the New Testament is astounding indeed.

Promise of the Messiah:

- Therefore the Lord Himself shall give you a sign; Behold a virgin shall conceive, and bear a Son, and shall call His name Immanuel. - (Isaiah 7:14)

135

And His Name Shall be Called:

- For unto us a child is born, unto us a Son is given: and the government shall be upon His shoulder: and His name shall be called Wonderful, Counsellor, The mighty God, The everlasting Father, The Prince of Peace. - (Isaiah 9:6)
- Of the increase of *His* government and peace *there shall be* no end, upon the throne of David, and upon His kingdom, to order it, and to establish it with judgment and with justice from henceforth even for ever.... - (Isaiah 9:7)

Out of Bethlehem:

- But thou, Bethlehem Ephratah, *though* thou be little among the thousands of Judah, *yet* out of thee shall He come forth unto Me *that is* to be ruler in Israel; whose goings forth *have been* from of old, from everlasting. - (Micah 5:2)

The Messenger to Prepare the Way:

- Behold, I will send My messenger, and he shall prepare the way before Me: and the Lord, whom ye seek, shall suddenly come to His temple, even the Messenger of the covenant, Whom ye delight in: behold, He shall come, saith the Lord of hosts. - (Malachi 3:1)

Begotten Son:

- I will declare the decree: the Lord hath said unto Me, Thou *art* My Son; this day have I begotten Thee. - (Psalms 2:7)

Time of His Arrival:

- Know therefore and understand, *that* from the going forth of the commandment to restore and to build Jerusalem unto the Messiah the Prince *shall be* seven weeks, and threescore and two weeks.... - (Daniel 9:25)
- And after threescore and two weeks shall Messiah be cut off, but not for Himself: unto the end of the war desolations are determined.... - (Daniel 9:26)

The prophecies of the first coming were numerous, even to the exact time and place. Nevertheless, since the Church missed the revelation of the Trinity these many years, it can be understood why the first coming of the Messiah could be overlooked by the Jewish people.

Prophecies and Their Fulfillment:
Now, let's look at more of those Old Testament prophecies, but this time, along with their fulfillment in the New Testament.

- Rejoice greatly, O daughter of Zion; shout, O daughter of Jerusalem: behold, thy King cometh unto thee: He *is* just, and having salvation; lowly, and riding upon an ass, and upon a colt the foal of an ass. - (Zechariah 9:9)
- And they brought the colt to Jesus, and cast their garments on Him; and He sat upon him. - (Mark 11:7)

- I gave My back to the smiters, and My cheeks to them that plucked off the hair: I hid not My face from shame and spitting. - (Isaiah 50:6)
- Then did they spit in His face, and buffeted Him; and others smote *Him* with the palms of their hands, - (Matthew 26:67)

- All they that see Me laugh Me to scorn: they shoot out the lip, they shake the head, *saying*, He trusted on the Lord *that* He would deliver Him: let Him deliver Him, seeing He delighted in Him. - (Psalm 22:7, 8)
- And the people stood beholding. And the rulers also with them derided *Him*, saying, He saved others; let Him save Himself, if He be Christ, the chosen of God. - (Luke 23:35)

- They gave Me also gall for My meat; and in My thirst they gave Me vinegar to drink. - (Psalms 69:21)
- They gave Him vinegar to drink mingled with gall: ... and He would not drink. - (Matthew 27:34)

- He keepeth all His bones: not one of them is broken. - (Psalm 34:20)
- But when they came to Jesus, and saw that He was dead already, they brake not His legs: - (John 19:33)

The evidence of the Old Testament prophecies, coupled with the eyewitness account of the apostles, offers a forceful combination.

The Disciples and the Messiah:

The notion that the Messiah would die was not in the teachings of the Jews. He was a coming Savior, but He was also a King, and not someone to be humiliated and spat upon. Even His own disciples abandoned Him when the soldiers took Him captive. Yet, when He resurrected and appeared to them in a glorious body with the nail prints visible, they were caught unaware because they never truly understood His purpose.

We must remember that these men were also Jews. They had knowledge of the Messiah and the expectations of Him for His Second Coming. They had just recently witnessed the triumphant entry of Jesus into Jerusalem, and at that time they thought He was going to be crowned King of kings. No wonder they could not understand when Jesus talked about His death. No wonder they fled when Jesus was captured. In their way of thinking, the Messiah was going to be a Redeemer, not taken to prison, and certainly not put to death.

Jesus appeared to the disciples several times within the 40 days He remained on earth after the resurrection. This confirmed their conviction that Jesus was truly the Messiah. Then they watched Him as He ascended into the heavens. That experience in itself was enough to convince anyone who Jesus was, but ten days after the ascension, the Holy Ghost came to dwell in their hearts. All these events together produced more than enough evidence that Jesus was indeed God in the flesh.

How were the apostles able to recall what was recorded in the New Testament? A promise, made by Jesus, assured them that the Holy Ghost would bring to remembrance the things He said and did while on earth. In this way the apostles were able to formulate the writings for the New Testament.

- But the Comforter, *which is* the Holy Ghost, whom the Father will send in My name, He shall teach you all things, and bring all things to your remembrance, whatsoever I have said unto you. - (John 14:26)

Summary of Chapter Twelve:

This chapter gives evidence that the Trinity is not just a New Testament idea. God began working on redemption from the very beginning when He said to Satan in the "Garden":

- And I will put enmity between thee and the woman, and between thy seed and her seed; it shall bruise thy head, and thou shalt bruise his heel. - (Genesis 3:15)

Throughout the Old Testament God told of the coming Messiah. However, it come to pass that man took control of the teachings and made them fit his design. After man added his version to the teachings, the *Truth* was lost. The result—the people missed the first coming and even crucified the Messiah.

The Scripture reference from the book of Psalms 2:7 presents an interesting disclosure, "... Thou *art* My Son; this day have I begotten Thee." As we have noted, every man is an offspring of the created being Adam. No created being has ever been begotten of God—man is begotten of man. The only one this verse can apply to is Jesus.

Chapter 13

Statements of Jesus

Jesus and His Ministry:
The Scriptures record many statements made by Jesus during His time on earth. Some have to do with His position in the Godhead, while others have to do with His claim to salvation. As mentioned earlier, these statements require humanity to make a decision about accepting or rejecting what He said as truth. With that concern, it would be fitting for us to investigate what Jesus really said.

The earthly ministry of Christ began at His baptism by John the Baptist. This is where the approval of the Father and the anointing by the Holy Ghost occurred. Immediately afterwards, the Spirit led Him into the wilderness where He fasted and prayed for forty days, and then He was tempted by the devil.

Jesus began proclaiming the Kingdom of God, and the need to repent and believe the gospel. His fame increased throughout the region, and men flocked to Him for healing and to hear His message. As He progressed in His ministry, His teachings became more focused as His audience consisted primarily of His disciples. At one point in the ministry of Jesus, the religious leaders sent officers to capture Him. The report, which they brought back, summarized the authority and wisdom by which Jesus spoke. In the report the officers said, "Never man spake like this Man" John 7:46.

Scriptures Relating to His Deity:

As we have seen, Jesus retained His deity while on earth. Our next passage from Matthew's gospel, supports that fact:

* And, behold, they brought to Him a man sick of the palsy, lying on a bed: and Jesus seeing their faith said unto the sick of the palsy; Son, be of good cheer; thy sins be forgiven thee. And, behold, certain of the scribes said within themselves, This *man* blasphemeth. And Jesus knowing their thoughts said, Wherefore think ye evil in your hearts? For whether is easier, to say, *Thy* sins be forgiven thee; or to say, Arise, and walk? But that ye may know that the Son of man hath power on earth to forgive sins, (then saith He to the sick of the palsy,) Arise, take up thy bed, and go unto thine house. And he arose and departed to his house. - (Matthew 9:2-7)

This is one of the works that testified the verification of His deity. While He did not directly say He was God, the things He said, and did, gave documentation to that fact.

Other Scriptures Maintain Deity:

Exodus 34:14 declares that God alone is to be worshipped. Nevertheless, Jesus was worshipped by angels, shepherds, wise men and others.

He had power over the wind and the sea:

* And He saith unto them, Why are ye fearful, O ye of little faith? Then He arose, and rebuked the winds and the sea; and there was a great calm. - (Matthew 8:26)

Power over demons:

* Saying, Let us alone; what have we to do with Thee, *Thou* Jesus of Nazareth? art Thou come to destroy us? I know Thee who Thou art; the Holy One of God. - (Luke 4:34)

- And Jesus rebuked him, saying, Hold thy peace, and come out of him. And when the devil had thrown him in the midst, he came out of him and hurt him not. - (Luke 4:35)

Power over disease:
- And He stood over her, and rebuked the fever; and it left her: and immediately she arose and ministered unto them. - (Luke 4:39)

The Angels of Jesus:
The next two Scriptures reveal that the angels belong to Jesus. Our first verse is taken from the parable of *the wheat and the tares*, and it tells us that Jesus is the Son of man. Furthermore, it discloses that He shall send *His angels*, to gather out of *His kingdom*, all things that are offensive. The second verse again maintains that the angels belong to the Son of man. Not only that, but it also reveals the Second Coming of Christ.

- The Son of man shall send forth **His angels**, and they shall gather out of **His kingdom** all things that offend, and them which do iniquity; - (Matthew 13:41)

- And then shall they see the Son of man coming in the clouds with great power and glory. And then He shall send **His angels**.... - (Mark 13:26, 27)

Jesus Said He is the Christ:
Jesus acknowledges that He is the Christ and Son of the Blessed. He again predicts His Second Coming.

- ...Again the high priest asked Him, and said unto Him, **Art Thou the Christ, the Son of the Blessed? And Jesus said, I am**: and ye shall see the Son of man sitting on the right hand of power, and coming in the clouds of heaven. - (Mark 14:61, 62)

Jesus Acknowledges He is the Messiah:

Jesus met a woman at Jacob's well whom He asked for water. Jesus admitted to her that He is the Messiah.

- The woman saith unto Him, I know that Messias cometh, which is called Christ: when He is come, He will tell us all things. **Jesus saith unto her, I that speak unto thee am He.** - (John 4:25, 26)

Jesus and His Relationship with the Father:

Next, we find some of the statements concerning Christ's position to the Father as well as His position in the Godhead.

Deny or confess Jesus among men:

This passage describes a requirement of man regarding Christ.

- Whosoever therefore shall confess Me before men, him will I confess also before My Father which is in heaven. But whosoever shall deny Me before men, him will I also deny before My Father which is in heaven. - (Matthew 10:32, 33)

Men should honor the Son:

Our next verse notes that the Son is to be given equal honor, such as that designated to the Father.

- All *men* should honour the Son, even as they honour the Father. He that honoureth not the Son honoureth not the Father which hath sent Him. - (John 5:23)

He came from heaven:

This verse strengthens an earlier statement that Jesus is not of the earth, but of heaven.

- For I came down from heaven, not to do Mine own will, but the will of Him that sent Me. - (John 6:38)

Jesus is One With the Father:
The following verses are direct statements, verifying Christ's deity and position in the Godhead.

- I and *My* Father are one. - (John 10:30)

- Neither pray I for these alone, but for them also which shall believe on Me through their word; That they all may be one; as Thou, Father, *art* in Me, and I in Thee, that they also may be one in Us.... - (John 17:20, 21)

Believe and See the Father:
The next two Scriptures further express how Jesus and the Father are one.

- Jesus cried and said, He that believeth on Me, believeth not on Me, but on Him that sent Me. And he that seeth Me seeth Him that sent Me. - (John 12:44, 45)

- Jesus saith unto him, Have I been so long time with you, and yet hast thou not known Me, Philip? he that hath seen Me hath seen the Father; and how sayest thou *then*, Show us the Father? - (John 14:9)

Statements of Salvation:
Jesus made many statements regarding His claim to salvation. These claims place a burden of decision upon the non-believer and his belief of Christ's position in the Godhead.

Everlasting Life:
To have everlasting life is to believe on Christ. The implication is to trust in Him alone for your salvation.

- Verily, verily, I say unto you, He that believeth on Me hath everlasting life. - (John 6:47)

Ye Shall Die In Your Sins:

This verse of Scripture is straightforward and one that must be evaluated with eternity in mind.

- I said therefore unto you, that ye shall die in your sins: for if ye believe not that I am *He*, ye shall die in your sins. - (John 8: 24)

Way, Truth and Life:

The next verse has caused much controversy over the years. As mentioned earlier, if Jesus was a messenger of God, then God is the one Who originated this statement:

- I am the Way, the Truth, and the Life: no man cometh unto the Father, but by Me. - (John 14:6)

Only One Way:

Jesus said: we cannot get there but through the door.

- Verily, verily, I say unto you, He that entereth not by the door into the sheepfold, but climbeth up some other way, the same is a thief and a robber. - (John 10:1)
- I am the door: by Me if any man enter in, he shall be saved and shall go in and out, and find pasture. - (John 10:9)

Summary of Chapter Thirteen:

We have looked at some of the Scripture passages from the Gospels relating to the deity of Christ. Some of the statements spoken by Jesus concerned not only His claim to be the Messiah, but also His equality with the Father. These statements are a challenge to the non-believer, requiring him to make a choice to either accept or reject Christ into his life.

Chapter 14

The Revelation of the Trinity

Questions and Truth:
Anyone at all acquainted with the Trinity is fully aware of its shrouded image. For the most part, the Trinity has produced numerous questions. How could it be that God the Father was in heaven, while God the Son was walking on the earth? How come the word Trinity is not presented in Scripture? How can Jesus be both God and Man? Over time, these questions proved difficult to explain because practical answers were never provided. This reality added much confusion, and in due course, the Trinity acquired the labeled of a mystery.

All Shall be Revealed:
The Bible clearly indicates "...there is nothing covered that shall not be revealed; and hid that shall not be known" Matthew 10:26. Our goal in this chapter is to track down and identify the neglected element that has placed a cloud over the Trinity and labeled it a mystery. We shall find that in revealing this element we also remove the mystery. However, as the above passage informs us, this element was never covered or hidden, only overlooked.

The Birth of Christ, A Different Look:
Needless to say, the events surrounding the birth of Christ were of the utmost importance. Therefore, in view of the Trinity, we want to explore what transpired from a different angle.

What was the unique characteristic about the birth of Christ? For one thing, it marked the first time that a woman was impregnated by anyone other than an heir of Adam. The implanted seed was not of an earthly being, but of a heavenly Being. In addition, the Body produced from that seed was pure, unstained and without the sin-nature of man. The same way man is prevented from connecting spiritually to God through Adam, Jesus was prevented from doing so through the family tree of Mary. Despite that, Jesus united with His Father through the Holy Ghost, and instead of being created of an earthly element (dust), He was fashioned of a heavenly element.

Bear in mind that any earthly substance is an impure substance. If Jesus would have been fashioned of an earthly substance, He would be an imperfect being. Only a pure seed could qualify for redemption. Still that seed had to be produced through the womb of a woman to qualify as a Human Being. In addition, He must be spiritually connected to God, but without a connection to Adam's ancestry because of the sin-nature.

We must also consider that any seed of mortal man that impregnates a woman is an impure seed. The man has attained the age of sin by the time he is ready for fatherhood. Only the pure seed of the Holy Ghost could produce the sinless Man needed to redeem mankind.

It is important to understand the significance of the pure seed and how it was produced. If that seed was not pure or if produced in any other way, Jesus would not be eligible to stand in the gap and pave the way for our redemption. It also helps to see that man is not a perfect being even though he could have lived forever except for sin. It is the Spirit of God connected to the spirit of man that allows for eternal life, and without that connection there is no life. Now let's look at something of a different nature.

Three Individuals:

It would be beneficial, at this point, to consider three situations concerning three individuals. We named them individual #1, individual #2 and individual #3.

#1. This sincere individual promises his child a trip to the zoo this weekend, but when the time arrives, something happens to prevent him from keeping his promise.

#2. This second individual promises his child a trip to the zoo with no intention of keeping his promise.

#3. This third individual promises his child a trip to the zoo and nothing will prevent him from keeping his promise.

In this illustration, individual #3 can be trusted, and his child will be satisfied. It is also possible that *if* both individuals #1 and #2 come up with good excuses, they too may satisfy their child's displeasure. Now let's say #1 and #2 again promise to take their children to the zoo the following weekend. Still, when next weekend comes, the same situation occurs along with more excuses. Certainly, each child would again be disappointed. So, following more excuses, both individuals again promise for the next weekend and again both fail for the third time to keep their promise. Chances are each child will gradually begin to lose trust in the one making the promises. As the broken promises continue, the trust diminishes even more.

Once our trust is lost, it is hard to regain. What we say, is directly related to how we are received. If we continually lie, we cannot be trusted. If we do not keep our word, it becomes worthless. Our word is who we are. What we say reveals our true worth. The Bible reveals the importance of our words.

- But I say unto you, That every idle word that men shall speak, they shall give account thereof in the day of judgment. - (Matthew 12:36)

Man is known by what he says, he is judged by others through his words. What Jesus reveals about the words we speak makes what we say of even greater importance.

The Element and the Word:

There are many words ascribed to Jesus in the Scriptures. He is referred to as Anointed, Beloved, Branch, Bread of Life, Cornerstone, Good Shepherd, Holy One of Israel, Mighty God, Rabbi, Rock, Rod, Savior, Son of God, Son of man, Wonderful and more. Yet, of all the names, only one describes the element employed to form Him as a Human Being.

Did God simply make Jesus from nothing? Certainly not. There was a definite element devised by God the Father to formulate God the Son. Just as man was made from the *dust* of the earth, Jesus also was made of a substance. What is that substance? What heavenly element did God use to make Jesus? The complete description of this mysterious element can be found in the first chapter of the gospel of John.

- In the beginning was the Word, and the Word was with God, and the Word was God. - (John 1:1)
- The same was in the beginning with God. - (John 1:2)
- All things were made by Him; and without Him was not anything made that was made. - (John 1:3)

When we think of Jesus as the Word of God, we look at Him as conveying to us what God wants us to know. Yes, He was conveying what God wanted Him to say. Yes, we can call Him a prophet, a messenger or teacher, but in reality, He is the Word of God. Here is what we must keep in mind. The very Word of God was the seed of the Holy Ghost that impregnated Mary. In other words, the seed devised to produce Jesus was God's very own Word. Now that we have identified the element of the seed, let's take a closer look at this element.

Where Words Originate:

When God said let there be—there was. Life issues forth from Him. God did not think the worlds into existence; He spoke and it was so. There is something about the spoken word. In the case with man, words can be poison, or they can be a blessing. They can cause wars, or they can make peace. The following passage is a portrayal of these facts:

- Not that which goeth into the mouth defileth a man; but that which cometh out of the mouth, this defileth a man. - (Matthew 15:11)

Man has a sin-nature, which speaks evil things that defile him. The book of James reports that no man can tame the tongue. What we feel inside is what we speak with our mouth.

Jesus said, "...how can ye, being evil, speak good things? **for out of the abundance of the heart the mouth speaketh.**" Matthew 12:34. This verse describes exactly where our words originate. Thus, we see that the words, which come out of the mouth, are first born in the heart. When they come out of the mouth, they are the element that defiles the man.

As presented in an earlier chapter, recall that man was the only creature made in the image and likeness of God. The desire of God is to enjoy the fellowship with someone like Himself. Searching the Scriptures, we find many similarities between God and man. Among those similarities, we notice where God is laughing, in another passage He was grieved in His heart, while another says He is a jealous God. We find that God has hands, eyes, back parts, a face, a mouth and a voice. Therefore, if the words of man originate in his heart, the words of God must originate in the heart of God. The following Scripture gives us an illustration of the heart of God:

- And the LORD smelled a sweet savour; **and the LORD said in His heart**, I will not again curse the ground any more for man's sake; for the imagination of man's heart *is* evil from his youth.... - (Genesis 8:12)

Hence, we must conclude that the Word of God is born in the heart of God. The voice of God utters the words, and the words are spoken with the mouth. Notice the voice is not the Word of God, but it utters the words. The mouth is not the Word of God; it is the instrument used to vocalize the words. The heart of God is where the words of God originate.

Man's Words are Eternal:
As you can see, the heart of God is truly the Word of God. What does that mean? Well, consider this: What would be the most important part of man? Every part of man remains on this earth to go back to the dust of the ground at death. Everything, that is, except his words. Words are a part of man that will follow him into eternity; or, as depicted in Matthew 12:36, at least until judgment day.

The words spoken by man come from the abundance of his heart. Similarly, the words spoken by God come from the abundance of the heart of God. It follows: If the heart is the vital part of man, then the heart is the vital part of God.

The Word Always Existed:
When God spoke the worlds into existence in chapter one of Genesis, He employed His Word. That Word was Jesus then, even though He was not incarnate at the time. Certainly, it is true; the Word of God always existed with the Father.

The Word from Heaven:
- For I came down from heaven, not to do mine own will, but the will of Him that sent Me. - (John 6:38)

Connection With Man:

Another item of interest involves the question of Jesus's connection with man. Did Jesus have a physical connection with mankind? The genealogies found in the gospels of Matthew and Luke tends to indicate that He did. Still, after a closer look, neither genealogy actually begets Jesus to man. These genealogies belong to Mary and Joseph and show their lineage to David, Abraham or Adam. We must note that even though Mary was chosen as the vessel to incarnate God's Word she also had to be His only connection to man. Mary's purpose truly was to bring Jesus into the world as a Human Being.

Why was it important for Jesus not to have a physical connection to mankind? One reason is that any physical connection to man also means a connection to Adam. If Jesus had a connection to Adam's ancestry, He would have inherited a sin-nature as well. Moreover, He would have acquired contaminated blood, inherent to every mortal being, which would not be fit for the atonement. Thus, it was imperative that the pure seed of the Holy Ghost be untainted in every way.

Words are not Tangible:

Because words are not a tangible substance, we tend to think that they could not be used as an element to impregnate the womb of a woman. At first glance, with our physical eyes, this prognosis makes sense. Nevertheless, it must be pointed out that words are a spiritual element; that is, they originate from the heart (spirit). Our separation from God was not physical, but spiritual. Man needed a spiritual connection back to God.

Adam disobeyed God when he ate of the forbidden fruit. Hence, the soul of man sinned by way of the flesh. It is the soul that needs redemption and not the spirit. The spirit goes back to God who gave it. If the spirit had sin on it, it could not go back to God. Still, the soul can only receive life through the spirit.

Other than our thoughts, words are the only component that comes from the spirit part of man by which we are able to associate. Accordingly, Jesus, who was made of the Word of God, is our spiritual connection back to God. The only conclusion for the possible redemption of man was by way of the spiritual substance—*the Word of God.*

The Words Belong to the Father:

John 14:24 clearly indicates that the Word does not belong to Jesus, but to the Father.

* He that loveth Me not keepeth not My sayings: and **the Word which ye hear is not mine, but the Father's** which sent Me. - (John 14:24)

Now, let's revisit some of those Scripture verses regarding Jesus and His relationship with the Father.

* ... no man knoweth the Son, but the Father; neither knoweth any man the Father, save the Son.... - (Matthew 11:27)

* ...I am the way, the truth, and the life: no man cometh unto the Father, but by Me. - (John 14:6)

* I and *My* Father are one. - (John 10:30)

* ...he that hath seen Me hath seen the Father.... - (John 14:9)

* ...My Father is greater than I. - (John 14:28)

Now We Know Why:

Now we know why, if you deny Jesus, you deny the Father.
Now we know why Jesus said, "My Father is greater than I."
Now we know why no man comes to the Father but by Jesus.

The Word Was Made Flesh:

- And the Word was made flesh, and dwelt among us, (and we beheld His glory, the glory as of the only begotten of the Father,) full of grace and truth. - (John 1:14)

The very Word of God was made flesh. Scripture points out His humanity: He wept, He slept, He was tempted, He hungered, He thirsted, and He bled. Then again, Scripture points out His divinity: He calmed the seas, He was worshipped as God, He knew their thoughts, and He had power over death.

The Suffering of the Father:

It seems that every detail concerning the redemption of man was carefully thought out. When we consider Jesus and the suffering He endured to redeem fallen man, we find that the Father was also affected. The heart of the Father must have been grieving, not only for the suffering of His Son, but also for sinful man and man's cruel disposition.

When we look at the Word of God as being the heart of God, we understand how much He truly loves us. If ever it could be said that God has a best part, we would have to conclude that He truly did care enough to give His best.

If there *is* a mystery connected to the Trinity, it is this: How could God love sinful man as He does?

Summary of Chapter Fourteen:

In this chapter, we tracked down and identified the element contained in the seed implanted in the womb of the Virgin Mary by the Holy Ghost. That substance was found to be the Word of God. We determined that the Word of God is really the heart of God, and, within the framework of this element, the mystery of the Trinity evolved.

Words defile a man, but the Word of God is pure. It contains no lie or deceit. The pure Word of God is also the same substance devised to produce the pure man (Jesus). If the words of man come from the abundance of his heart, we must conclude that the words of God come from the heart of God. Interestingly, Jesus (the Son of God) is the center of the Trinity and Jesus (the heart of God) is the center of the Father.

Without question, we have barely touched the surface regarding the Trinity. As the apostle John stated:

- And there are also many other things which Jesus did, the which, if they should be written every one, I suppose that even the world itself could not contain the books that should be written. Amen. - (John 21:25)

In Conclusion:

We have touched on many areas regarding the Trinity in our study. Certainly this revelation will help clarify many areas of confusion we may have had. Questions relating to the Virgin Birth and those regarding Mary as the mother of God should be less disputable. Many Scripture verses regarding Jesus should become more understandable. You may even have a different outlook regarding the questions of: "Who am I, why was I made and where am I going after I die?" Yet, first and foremost, the unveiling of the Trinity and the revelation of the fullness of the Godhead was our most significant discovery.

Who God is and what He did to secure our freedom from sin and Satan cannot be undermined. Yes, there is a day coming when Jesus (the Messiah) will be crowned King of kings and Lord of lords. Multitudes who have traveled down this pathway, called life, will be in attendance on that day. Another multitude will not attend; yet, not because they were not invited but because they exercised their free will and rejected Christ.

The alternative to salvation is dreadful, yet avoidable. The allotted time of each individual on earth is as a final exam. The peculiarity of this exam is that there is only one question and only one answer.

For Our Readers: As you can see, Jesus did not die solely for one particular group of people, but for the world. If you are one of the billions spoken of in the very first paragraph of our study, you are included as one of those for whom Christ died.

When it comes your turn to disembark this earth, all of your worldly possessions will remain, but you will depart. The choice you made regarding salvation will become your final answer. Your eternal destination will be settled forever.

Only you can make the decision. If you have not taken the challenge offered in the sixth chapter of this book under the heading of "born-again," now would be a good time to do so.

For Our Leaders: The mystery is now history. The hour of decision has come for the Church. What will we do with the information contained in this book? Should we incorporate this information with the data already available regarding the Trinity, or shall we continue to refer to the Trinity as a mystery? Will we construct a solid foundation for the next generation of leaders, or shall we leave them with the same dogma that dumfounded the Church for the last 1800 years?

We can suffocate the evangelism of the Church with our confusion, or we can prove our way into the hearts of those searching for answers. The next step belongs to you. May God guide and bless each and everyone.

To Order:

The Unveiling of the Trinity
by Tom Bosse

Quanity: Total:

_____   "The Unveiling of the Trinity" $_____
A composite look at the concept of the Trinity.

ISBN 0-9723974-0-X $12.95 Each

Indicate quanity and total above. Fill out below.
send to:

Tuvott Publishing   **Order Total: $**_____
PO Box 18276
Erlanger, KY 41018-0276   **Shipping:**   **$**_____

                                        ($3.50 for 1 Book)
Name_____   (add .75 for each
                                        additional Book)
Address_____   **[Note: No Additional
                                        Shipping Charges
City_____   Over 5 Books.|**

State_____**Zip**_____   **Total Due: $**_____
                                        (Payable in US Funds Only)

☐ **Payment Enclosed (Check or Money Order Only)**   **(No Cash Orders Accepted)**

No Credit Cards by Mail.
For Credit Cards: Go To Web-Site: www.tuvott.com

PLEASE ALLOW 2-4 WEEKS FOR DELIVERY.
For Quanity Orders Please Write or go to Web-Site.
Phone: 859 341-6004   Fax: 859 341-6033